C000298867

THE UPPER ROOM

DAILY MEDITATIONS FROM AROUND THE WORLD

Stephen D. Bryant
Editor and Publisher

INTERDENOMINATIONAL
INTERNATIONAL
INTERRACIAL

76 EDITIONS
40 LANGUAGES

The Upper Room
May–August 2010
Edited by Susan Hibbins

The Upper Room © BRF 2010
The Bible Reading Fellowship
15 The Chambers, Vineyard, Abingdon OX14 3FE
Tel: 01865 319700; Fax: 01865 319701
Email: enquiries@brf.org.uk
Website: www.brf.org.uk
BRF is a Registered Charity

ISBN 978 1 84101 753 2

Acknowledgments

The New Revised Standard Version of the Bible, Anglicized Edition, copyright © 1989, 1995 by the Division of Christian Education of the National Council of the Churches of Christ in the USA. Used by permission. All rights reserved.

The Holy Bible, New International Version, copyright © 1973, 1978, 1984 by International Bible Society. Used by permission of Hodder & Stoughton Publishers, a member of the Hachette Livre UK Group. All rights reserved. 'NIV' is a registered trademark of International Bible Society. UK trademark number 1448790.

Extracts from the Authorised Version of the Bible (The King James Bible), the rights in which are vested in the Crown, are reproduced by permission of the Crown's Patentee, Cambridge University Press.

Scriptures quoted from the Good News Bible published by The Bible Societies/HarperCollins Publishers Ltd, UK © American Bible Society 1966, 1971, 1976, 1992, used by permission.

Printed in the UK by HSW Print.

The Upper Room: how to use this book

The Upper Room is ideal in helping us spend a quiet time with God each day. Each daily entry is based on a passage of scripture, and is followed by a meditation and prayer. Each person who contributes a meditation to the magazine seeks to relate their experience of God in a way that will help those who use The Upper Room every day.

Here are some guidelines to help you make best use of The Upper Room:

1. Read the passage of Scripture. It is a good idea to read it more than once, in order to have a fuller understanding of what it is about and what you can learn from it.
2. Read the meditation. How does it relate to your own experience? Can you identify with what the writer has outlined from their own experience or understanding?
3. Pray the written prayer. Think about how you can use it to relate to people you know, or situations that need your prayers today.
4. Think about the contributor who has written the meditation. Some Upper Room users include this person in their prayers for the day.
5. Meditate on the 'Thought for the Day', the 'Link2Life' and the 'Prayer Focus', perhaps using them again as the focus for prayer or direction for action.

Why is it important to have a daily quiet time? Many people will agree that it is the best way of keeping in touch every day with the God who sustains us, and who sends us out to do his will and show his love to the people we encounter each day. Meeting with God in this way reassures us of his presence with us, helps us to discern his will for us and makes us part of his worldwide family of Christian people through our prayers.

I hope that you will be encouraged as you use the magazine regularly as part of your daily devotions, and that God will richly bless you as you read his word and seek to learn more about him.

Susan Hibbins
UK Editor

In Times of/For Help with . . .

Below is a list of entries in this copy of *The Upper Room* relating to situations or emotions with which we may need help:

Anger: May 16

Anxiety: May 25, 27; June 1, 18, 24; July 16, 23; Aug 21

Assurance: May 17; July 12, 21, 30; Aug 13, 16, 26

Bible reading: May 14, 21, 26, 28; June 6, 29; July 1, 12, 16, 18, 21; Aug 15, 28

Caring for our world: Aug 2, 16

Celebration: May 1, 10

Change: May 14, 25; June 2, 5, 10, 19, 28; July 13, 23; Aug 8

Christian community: May 6, 14, 23, 30; July 4, 7, 17; Aug 5, 11, 15, 22, 31

Christian unity: May 19; July 4

Creation/Nature's beauty: May 24; June 4, 12, 23; July 12, 21, 29; Aug 2, 4, 10

Death: July 11, 20; Aug 20, 26

Doubt: Aug 15, 22

Failure: May 25; July 15, 27, 31; Aug 19

Faith: July 23

Fear: June 18; July 5, 16; Aug 11

Forgiving: May 7, 16, 22; June 13; July 15, 27, 29, 31

Friendship: May 17, 19, 23; July 7, 17, 19, 20; Aug 5, 15, 22

Generosity/Giving: May 8, 15, 21, 22, 29; June 8; July 6, 14, 20

God's grace: July 15; Aug 3

God's love: May 21, 24, 29; June 2, 3, 7; July 15, 21, 25; Aug 8, 16, 19, 20

God's mercy: July 15, 31; Aug 23, 29

God's power: May 12; June 14, 21, 27

God's presence: May 9, 24; June 3, 10, 22; July 11, 28; Aug 8, 22, 26, 31

God's provision: July 16, 20, 28; Aug 3

God's will: May 4, 7, 18; Aug 5, 7

Gratitude: May 10, 22; July 28; Aug 12

Grief: May 17, 30; June 22, 28; Aug 14

Guidance: May 12, 18, 24, 28; June 5, 16, 25, 29; July 13, 18; Aug 5, 7, 13, 28

Healing/Illness: May 9, 12, 17; July 4, 5; Aug 3, 20, 24, 26, 27, 30, 31

Hope: July 28, 30, 31; Aug 26

Hunger: July 6, 24; Aug 14

Job issues: May 11, 16; July 2, 10, 16

Judging: May 2, 19

Loneliness: June 22, 28

Loss: May 12, 17, 25, 30; June 24, 28; July 16; Aug 20

Materialism: June 1, 8

Mission: June 10, 17, 26; Aug 1, 21

New beginnings: May 7, 16, 28; June 17, 19; July 31; Aug 19, 24, 27

Obedience: May 28; June 9, 15, 17; July 12, 13; Aug 1, 2, 7, 14, 20, 23, 28

Parenting: May 2, 9, 26; June 18, 20; July 9, 15; Aug 27, 29

Peace: July 5, 7; Aug 22, 28

Prayer: May 2, 12, 31; June 2, 30; July 1, 5, 16, 18, 28; Aug 5, 7, 13, 25, 28

Rest/Sabbath: July 10

Salvation: May 7, 17, 28; June 7, 9, 13; July 2, 27, 30, 31

Serving: May 11, 13, 15; June 2, 15, 20, 23, 26; July 6, 8, 10, 11, 20; Aug 1, 4, 9

Sharing faith: June 13, 15, 23; July 9, 25; Aug 6, 11, 14, 17, 19, 21, 23, 30

Social issues: May 4, 23; June 8, 21; July 31, Aug 11, 14, 17, 18

Spiritual gifts: May 19, 23; June 2, 11, 15, 23; July 8; Aug 4, 9, 17, 21, 23

Spiritual practices: May 11, 13, 18, 20, 26, 28; June 6, 11

Stress: May 9, 12, 20, 31; June 3

Trust: May 9, 27; June 5, 10, 12, 14, 16, 18, 21, 25; July 16, 27, 28; Aug 30

4

One Family

The world that Jesus came into was a fractured mess like ours. It seems as though the people were divided into hostile and alienating groups. The occupying Romans were resented by their subjects; Jews would not dine with Samaritans; Sadducees and Pharisees vied for influence; zealots wanted to slit the throats of tax collectors. Then you had the accepted divides between rich and poor, men and women, young and old, not to mention a virtual partition between Jew and Gentile. The human family was in a mess!

And yet Jesus Christ breaks through this culture of hatred, a culture we ourselves know so well, with the amazing grace by which he comes back from the dead and calls his unfaithful and cowardly followers 'my brothers' (Matthew 28:10).

In the days of Pentecost, people saw a true miracle happening in the community of those who followed Jesus, the people of 'the Way' (Acts 9:2). They saw those who were supposed to hate each other actually caring for one another, obviously having forgiven their enemies. Those who weren't supposed to walk or eat together were seen sharing all things in common. They bore witness to a better way and to the power of God's love to turn enemies into not just friends but a new kind of family.

The Upper Room fellowship is a worldwide family of prayer that transcends all natural partitions: race, nation, sexuality, age, poverty and wealth, freedom or lack of it. It has been my joy and privilege to serve you and this fellowship as World Editor and Publisher for the past twelve years, the full tenure that is allowed. I invite you to join me in praying in this my final editorial, that each of you—wherever you are—will be living proof that there is a better way. Holy Spirit, 'make us one with Christ, one with each other', and bold witnesses to the amazing grace and boundary-breaking love of God.

Stephen D. Bryant
Editor and Publisher

The Editor writes...

I was watching one of the leading snooker players, Stephen Hendry, as he compiled what would become a maximum 147 break. As he steadily potted the red and black balls, the commentators started to focus excitedly on the pink ball, one of the last colours to be potted, which was lying in an awkward position on the table. Trying to increase the tension of the moment, the commentators drew attention constantly to the difficult pink ball, expecting that it would present a real problem in a few minutes' time.

I thought that it was just as well that Stephen Hendry could not hear what they were saying. Although snooker players have to plan their shots in advance, when they pot a ball, their whole concentration needs to be on that one shot. If they are thinking too far ahead, very often they miss the shot right in front of them.

Jesus is the perfect example of how to deal carefully with one thing at a time. In all his encounters with people in the gospels there is no sense of rush or hurry, or of talking to someone with one eye on the next person who was seeking his help. Jesus dealt with one person or situation, and then went on to concentrate on the next. Even when he was on his way to see Jairus' daughter, he stopped because he realised that someone had touched him in the crowd. Unhurriedly he then gave his full attention to the woman whose faith had healed her from a long illness, while Jairus no doubt waited in a fever of impatience beside him. Jairus' fear and panic was turned to joy when Jesus then restored his daughter to life (Mark 5:21–43).

As for the future, and how difficult it might be, Jesus gave us the antidote to worrying about it: 'Can any of you by worrying add a single hour to your span of life?' (Matthew 6:27). Keeping our eyes firmly on Jesus, and on what is happening at the moment, gives us no time to worry about what might happen at some time in the future.

(Just for the record, Stephen Hendry had no trouble in potting the pink.)

Susan Hibbins
Editor of the UK edition

PS: The Bible readings are selected with great care, and we urge you to include the suggested reading in your devotional time.

Every Day is a Good Day

Read Psalm 118:19–24

This is the day the Lord has made; let us rejoice and be glad in it.
Psalm 118:24 (NIV)

It began as a normal day and continued to be normal. It was about as routine as any of my recent days had been. For almost four months, circumstances brought about by the illness of my wife of 54 years had determined the course of my days and the activities in them. So, throughout the day, I followed the usual routine. Among the many things I wanted and needed to do, I gave my attention to what I had to do.

At the close of that day, I reflected upon its events. Although I thought of it as an ordinary day with little more than routine events, an inescapable thought formed in my mind and would not go away: *Above everything else, this has been a good day*!

As those words rushed into my mind, the words of a Hebrew poet joined them: 'This is the day the Lord has made; let us rejoice and be glad in it' (Psalm 118:24).

No day is ever ordinary, for every day is a good day—a valuable gift given to us by the Maker of days. Therefore, each day is to be used wisely, enjoyed fully and appreciated genuinely.

Prayer: *Giver of this good day, thank you for this gift. May we use it wisely. We pray in the name of our Lord Jesus Christ. Amen*

Thought for the Day: Today is a gift from the Maker of days. I will rejoice in it.

Howard Coop (Kentucky)

A Call to Pray

Read 1 Timothy 2:1–4

First of all, then, I urge that supplications, prayers, intercessions, and thanksgivings be made for everyone.
1 Timothy 2:1 (NRSV)

In an effort to make myself and my family more aware of the needs of those around us, I have made it my habit to pray for those affected by pain or tragedy when we see an ambulance pass. My children have earnestly latched on to this idea and remind me if I do not notice.

One day my three-year-old saw a police officer by the roadside speaking to someone he had pulled over. 'Mummy, we need to pray for them!' she exclaimed.

I was poised to say, 'No, darling, that person isn't sick or hurt. He just broke a rule', when I realised that the driver also needed our prayers. For that matter, so did the police officer! I realised in a fresh way that there isn't a soul on earth who does not need to be lifted up to God in prayer. I inwardly shifted my perspective and said, 'You are right! Let's pray.'

Prayer: *Gracious Father, open our eyes to the myriad opportunities we have each day to pray for others. In Jesus' name. Amen*

Thought for the Day: Who needs my prayers today?

Link2Life: *Today, let signs of distress remind you to pray.*

Heather Davis (Tennessee)

PRAYER FOCUS: THOSE RECEIVING EMERGENCY MEDICAL CARE

My Sheep

Read John 10:11–15
The Lord is my shepherd; I shall not be in want.
Psalm 23:1 (NIV)

When on holiday in Cyprus we watched a shepherd taking care of his sheep. It was a calm and memorable moment for us. The shepherd watched over his sheep; he walked slowly in front of the sheep—looking back at them constantly—and the sheep followed him trustingly. He didn't need to push or shove them; he didn't hit them with his staff. This reminded me of the words from Isaiah: 'He tends his flock like a shepherd: He gathers the lambs in his arms and carries them close to his heart; he gently leads those that have young' (Isaiah 40:11).

In Spanish the word for shepherd is *pastor*, and I like that image. I see my pastor as a caretaker for the flock, the people of our church. In this role he imitates Christ the Good Shepherd. I trust my pastor as my shepherd, and I recognise the authority God has given to him. It is not an easy role to fill, so I pray for our pastor daily, that he will lead the flock in the ways that God would have us go.

Prayer: *Good Shepherd, lead us to refreshing waters and good pasture, that we may live safely in your care. Strengthen all those who lead your people, that they may guide wisely and well. As Jesus taught us, we pray, 'Our Father which art in heaven, Hallowed be thy name. Thy kingdom come. Thy will be done in earth, as it is in heaven. Give us this day our daily bread. And forgive us our debts, as we forgive our debtors. And lead us not into temptation, but deliver us from evil: For thine is the kingdom, and the power, and the glory, for ever. Amen' (Matthew 6:9–13, KJV)*

Thought for the Day: We can trust God, our Shepherd, to lead us.

Josephine M. Sherard (Canary Islands, Spain)

A Different Standard

Read Amos 7:7–9
[God] who began a good work in you will carry it on to completion until the day of Christ Jesus.
Philippians 1:6 (NIV)

I love gadgets. So you can imagine my excitement when I saw the newest laser spirit-level on sale. Having just moved, I had pictures and wall hangings to be hung. This tool would do the trick! Minutes later, I was at home shooting the laser's little red beam on every flat surface of my house. (It even curved around corners.) I had confirmed within the hour that everything in my house was level. Content, I put the gadget on a shelf—where it still sits. The pictures and wall hangings remain unhung.

In today's reading from Amos, the prophet talks about a different levelling tool, a plumb line. The plumb line, a piece of string with a metal weight, is hung to see if vertical lines such as walls are straight (plumb). If they are not, with time walls may buckle. Amos says that a time is coming when all people will be measured according to God's standards. God is no longer content with the way the people have begun to buckle and sway.

God calls us all to be ready, to examine ourselves by the standard established through scripture and Christian tradition. Even if we leave these tools on a shelf to collect dust, God is faithful. Each of us is a project that God will see through to completion.

Prayer: *Holy God, give us courage to look at ourselves in the light of who you call us to be. Then help us to open ourselves to the transforming work of the Holy Spirit. Amen*

Thought for the Day: Make a list of the things God values. How do you measure up?

Bill Lizor (Tennessee)

Lighthouses

Read Matthew 5:13–16
You are a chosen race, a royal priesthood, a holy nation, God's own people, in order that you may proclaim the mighty acts of him who called you out of darkness into his marvellous light.
1 Peter 2:9 (NRSV)

Lighthouse keepers have to be a sturdy breed. It can be wearing and lonely to be stationed where they are. The work is generally heaviest when and where conditions are the worst. A lighthouse might be more comfortable stationed inland. But those in the riskiest locations—out there where the wind blows—have the most opportunities to rescue lives.

The glow of a lighthouse isn't meant to illuminate the inside of the building. It's meant to pierce obscurity when darkness descends and storms arise. The noise a lighthouse makes isn't for the keeper's entertainment. It's for cutting through fog too thick for light to penetrate, for raising an alarm, for guiding the lost.

When I see a lighthouse planted at the far edge of safety, I think of our call to be light to the world. Like the beacons that guide ships to safe harbour, we are the hope of the Lord made visible. We drive our light into the darkness and our voices through the fog of life. 'See! Hear! Come! Christ is where chaos ends.' Let us shine boldly so that those still tossing in the storm may find their way to the safe harbour that Christ offers.

Prayer: *Lord, give me your courage to be a light when darkness is overwhelming. Amen*

Thought for the Day: God calls us out of darkness, and makes us into light for others.

Teresa Murphy (Oregon)

The Fifth Voice

Read 1 Corinthians 13:4–7
Jesus said, 'By this everyone will know that you are my disciples, if you have love for one another.'
John 13:35 (NRSV)

Our minister was away today, and our local high-school music teacher preached. He spoke about 'the fifth voice', which I had never heard of. He drew the concept from the singing of barber-shop quartets. 'The fifth voice' refers to the one harmony created by the four voices as they join together in song. The unified sound becomes like a fifth voice.

Just as a group of singers can be more than each of them is alone, Christians living in love create something more than they could on their own. The day before Jesus was crucified, he told his disciples that the world would know that they were his followers by the way they related to one another. They were to cherish and care for one another.

1 Corinthians 13 describes the characteristics of this Christian love. Paul exhorted the Corinthians to be patient and kind, to turn aside from jealousy, boastfulness, pride, rudeness, selfishness and irritability. Love forgives and lets go of hurts and offences of the past. When Christians live together in love, the world hears a voice it needs to hear: the fifth voice that reveals the presence of the Saviour.

Prayer: *Dear God, fill us with love for our brothers and sisters in Christ. Amen*

Thought for the Day: The church is more than the sum of its parts.

Ted De Hass (Iowa)

Broken and Restored

Read Isaiah 61

Restore us, O God; make your face shine upon us, that we may be saved.
Psalm 80:3 (NIV)

I am an antique dealer, and I'm always energised by the process of rescuing and restoring a once-treasured article to its former condition and usefulness. Some of my projects need only a good cleaning or thorough polishing to bring them back to life, while others are cracked or broken and require major repairs. Each time I am able to restore an old treasure, I think about God's joy in directing the process of our restoration. As promised, God is making us and the entire creation whole (see Revelation 21:1–7.)

For me, restoration is the one-word message of the entire Bible. God is revealed as the absolute, divine Saviour. We less-than-perfect human beings with a tendency to continue living in our damaged state are the same as the antiques that I find—flawed, broken and in need of a new start.

Through God's compassionate work, we are given new life by faith in Jesus Christ, who was 'delivered over to death for our sins and was raised to life for our justification' (Romans 4:25). By faith in Christ, we become new creations, able to become all that God created us to be.

Prayer: *Thank you, Father, that through faith in Jesus Christ we are made whole. Amen*

Thought for the Day: God's one-word message to us is 'restoration'.

Sandra Bartz (Ohio)

The Widow's Offering

Read Mark 12:41–44
Blessed are the poor in spirit, for theirs is the kingdom of heaven.
Matthew 5:3 (NIV)

My church's annual gift-day appeal had come in the post and sat on my hall table for about a week. Each day as I came and went to work, I saw the envelope and thought about all the bills I had to pay and the conflict I felt about the spirit of my giving to the ministries of my church.

One morning I read the Bible story of the poor widow who gave generously in spite of her poverty, contributing all she had to live on, in faith that God would sustain her. Jesus recognised this gift as more precious than the offerings of the rich who gave out of their abundance.

I realised that we all come to Christ in spiritual poverty. We have nothing to offer in return for the gifts God gives us; we can only offer ourselves as servants to the will of God. God receives us and welcomes us into fullness of life. While supporting my church is an important part of my Christian calling, God does not desire offerings given out of obligation or ritual but out of my heart's love. Acknowledging my spiritual poverty before God has made me deeply grateful for all that I have and has opened my heart to support the work of my church and others in need.

Prayer: *Loving God, accept us in our spiritual poverty, and lead us to love and serve you with our whole heart. Amen*

Thought for the Day: How can I use faithfully the gifts that God has given me?

Michael Albanese (New York)

I Am with You

Read Psalm 130

Yea, though I walk through the valley of the shadow of death, I will fear no evil: for thou art with me.
Psalm 23:4 (KJV)

The doctor entered the room where I was keeping vigil over my son. An infection was raging through his body and had damaged his internal organs and heart. 'We're pumping in antibiotics; but if the infection reaches his brain, he won't make it through the night.'

I sat in shock. My 18-year-old son was going to die? I had never felt so alone or so helpless. My heart cried out to God. I willed God to speak to me. Gradually, peace and resolve came over me. Alone in the darkness, I trusted that no matter what happened, God would see me through it. I sat by the bed all night long, knowing that God was beside me.

My son made it through that night, but his recovery was slow and painful. He has a permanent disability because of his illness, but he is now finishing college and moving on with his life. Through it all, God has been with us.

That dark time in my life made me stronger. Now I realise that when I am weak, God will hold me up and walk with me through the valley.

Prayer: *O God, help us to know in our hearts that you are walking beside us at all times, seeing us through our lowest moments and answering our prayers before we speak. Amen*

Thought for the Day: God waits with us through our darkest nights.

Sue Constantinides (Maryland)

Where are the other nine?

Read Luke 17:11–19

Rejoice always, pray without ceasing, give thanks in all circumstances;
for this is the will of God in Christ Jesus for you.
1 Thessalonians 5:16–18 (NRSV)

We are taught from childhood to say thank you when we are given something or helped in some way. Yet having thanked someone once for a kindness shown us does not release us from responsibility to express our gratitude again for future kind acts. Even so, we often forget to thank family and friends for their help, concern, affection and attention, or for a tasty meal and a tender embrace.

We sometimes behave in a similar way toward God. In the Bible story about the ten lepers healed by Jesus, only one thanks his Healer. The other nine healings go unacknowledged. Perhaps that percentage applies to us. Maybe we forget nine times out of ten to notice and give thanks for the gifts of love in our lives. I can imagine Jesus standing before me, saying, 'You have thanked me for one miracle, for one answer to your prayer. But what about the other times?'

I don't want to take my blessings for granted. I want to have a sensitive and grateful heart; I want the people around me to know and hear that I value their part in my life, each small kindness that they show me. And I want to remember to thank God, too, for each good gift in my life. Each day we can pray to live with gratitude.

Prayer: *Lord Jesus, forgive us when we do not thank you for answering our prayers. Open our eyes to see your gifts when they come to us. Amen*

Thought for the Day: For what do I thank God today?

Julia Jefimtsuk (Harjumaa, Estonia)

Faithful Tentmakers

Read Acts 18:1–4
We are what he has made us, created in Christ Jesus for good works.
Ephesians 2:10 (NRSV)

Like other rabbis of his era, the apostle Paul was expected to support himself independent of his teaching in local synagogues. Paul's profession was tent making, and through that work he came to know people such as Aquila and Priscilla, who would become leaders in the early church.

Today we think of Paul as an extraordinary person—not because of his tent making but because of how he called people to follow Christ. Certainly there must have been days for Paul when making tents came first. I think of this sometimes when my everyday duties become priorities that seem distant from my focus on faith.

Paul's experience reminds me that in any good work I can find Christ and others who can be a part of my Christian experience. God can be glorified in how I handle the simplest chores and the most troublesome tasks. We can all be faithful in the work of helping others know, love and serve Christ.

Prayer: *Lord, may we glorify your name in all that we undertake each day. Amen*

Thought for the day: We can serve Christ in our daily tasks.

John Blossom (Connecticut)

Prayer Champion

Read Psalm 71:1–14

O God, do not be far from me; O my God, make haste to help me!
Psalm 71:12 (NRSV)

My grandmother was a champion at praying. She could pray for 20 minutes without taking a breath, and she seasoned her prayers liberally with unfamiliar-sounding words from the King James Bible. Her prayers were intimidating in scope, scale and content. However, when she suffered a series of strokes, her prayers became simple and direct. I held her hand in the hospital as she whispered, simply, 'O God, help me; O Jesus, comfort me.'

Like my grandmother, the psalmists model both eloquent praying and how to cut through fancy language to the heart of the matter. In the midst of lofty verses in the psalms, we often find the song of the heart: 'save me,' 'rescue me', 'hear me', 'do not forsake me'. God is the source of salvation, protection, comfort and victory in times of great need.

Psalm 71 shows us how Jesus might have prayed in his last week, knowing the great trials he would endure and finding solace and comfort in God's great power and grace. Jesus needed to feel God's presence and guiding hand that week in Jerusalem (see Luke 19—23). And when we struggle in uncertainty or pain, we can remember that for us as for Jesus, God is still 'a rock of refuge, a strong fortress'.

Prayer: *O Lord, be our refuge when the pressures and demands of life grow too great. Receive us, rescue us, and restore us, that we may share your praise and good news. Amen*

Thought for the Day: God wants us to tell him whatever is in our heart.

Dan R. Dick (Wisconsin)

Time Well Spent

Read Luke 10:38–42

[Jesus] said to [his disciples], 'Come away to a deserted place all by yourselves and rest a while.'
Mark 6:31 (NRSV)

A friend listened patiently as I rattled on about my busy day and my never-ending list of things to do. I felt I had used my time wisely, but her response surprised me.

'Where did God fit in?' she asked. Embarrassed, I realised I had expected to be praised for all my accomplishments. Her question made me re-evaluate my busy schedule.

Most of us want others to see us as industrious. Do we dare admit that we spend time praying or reading the Bible or that we simply sit and ponder God's blessings in our life?

Jesus wanted his disciples to serve; but more than that, he wanted relationships with them. In addition, Jesus invited them into times of rest to renew their minds and bodies for the work they were called to do.

We can easily fall into the trap of trying to impress others with our doing and overlook the importance of 'resting' time with God. With God on our daily calendar, we will find renewed energy to accomplish all that lies before us each day.

Prayer: *Heavenly Father, forgive us for trying to please you with our achievements. Draw us aside that we may be renewed by spending time in your presence. Amen*

Thought for the Day: How often do I rest in God's presence?

Link2Life: *Schedule time with God this week.*

Connie Coppings (Kentucky)

Growing Together

Read Romans 12:3–8

All these are the work of one and the same Spirit, and he gives them to each one, just as he determines.
1 Corinthians 12:11 (NIV)

I had doubts about accepting the invitation to join a men's Bible study group. I was busy enough already. Besides I did not know half the men in the group. All my reasons for not getting involved seemed justified and rational.

At first I felt reluctant to speak honestly and personally within the group. I felt vulnerable and lacked self-confidence. On my drive to the meetings, I wondered whether I was really supposed to be in the group. I left thinking that we only scratched the surface of certain issues, and I regretted that the group had not gone deeper.

But as our meetings continued, I found that I looked forward to going. I sensed that God was nudging me to change my perspective. When I heard others talk of challenges to their faith, I had a greater understanding and appreciation for their experience. I realised that I had a responsibility to talk about my experience and to be understood, challenged and loved.

Each member of the group brought different perspectives to our discussions. In many ways this group of men could not have been more diverse, yet God built for us a foundation of friendship, trust and spiritual growth.

Prayer: *Dear God, thank you for drawing us into new situations and relationships to help us grow in our faith. Grant us the ability to trust and encourage one another. Amen*

Thought for the Day: Growing in faith with others is part of God's plan.

Bruce W. Bunce (North Carolina)

None Too Small

Read John 6:1–13
'Here is a boy with five small barley loaves and two small fish, but how far will they go among so many?'
John 6:9 (NIV)

I manage a guesthouse in a seaside village in South Africa. There God has given me wonderful opportunities to encourage and witness to people from all walks of life and from all over the world. Sometimes I am able only to show warmth and kindness, or to speak an occasional word of understanding. However, people thank me as if I had given them a wonderful treasure. I used to be amazed and puzzled because I felt I had done so little.

Then the Holy Spirit opened my eyes. I realised that the Spirit magnifies each little kindness so that people receive the bounty of the Lord Jesus Christ, which is enormous. Seeing the look on the faces of my guests, I know that God is good and powerful.

As the little boy's offering of bread and fish fed five thousand, so God takes whatever we offer from the heart and uses it to feed many. Let us always offer even what seems small to us, for in so doing we show trust in our great and limitless God.

Prayer: *Dear Lord, thank you for taking our small offerings and using them in big ways. Help us never to hold back, thinking that what we offer is too small, but to give with an honest heart. In the name of Jesus Christ. Amen*

Thought for the Day: The Holy Spirit works through anything we do or say in love.

Elaine Richardson (Western Cape, South Africa)

Difficult Choices

Read Luke 22:31–34, 54–62

Be merciful to me, O God, because of your constant love… I recognise my faults; I am always conscious of my sins.
Psalm 51:1, 3 (GNB)

I feel sure that the apostle Peter often wished he'd kept his mouth shut and just walked away or that he'd reacted differently. Jesus warned Peter about the denials. And God warns us. But like Peter, we don't always listen.

I've lived long enough to have many regrets. Most of those involve words—usually harsh criticisms—that, despite my good intentions, never helped anyone.

I remember when I wounded someone a couple of years ago. We had served together in ministry to help others, but only recently did my colleague and I take the first step toward reconciliation. I'm glad we did. It wasn't easy for me, and it may not have been comfortable for her either. But she assured me that she bears no animosity. Such forgiveness is priceless. We both recognised that we can't change the past. Instead, we decided to move forward.

That's not always easy because, like Peter, we remember what we did. It's hard to forget and forgive. And sometimes we are least likely to forgive ourselves. We can't change what we've done, but we can change how we behave now. We can choose to think before we speak; we can choose to seek forgiveness from those we've hurt. And we can choose to forgive ourselves. These are not easy choices, but they are necessary.

Prayer: *O God, help us to forgive ourselves as we forgive others. Amen*

Thought for the Day: The evidence of repentance is behaving differently.

Jeff Adams (Arizona)

In Heaven

Read John 14:1–7

Our citizenship is in heaven, and it is from there that we are expecting a Saviour, the Lord Jesus Christ.
Philippians 3:20 (NRSV)

Andy's cancer diagnosis just ten months earlier had been shocking. Now he lay frighteningly still, barely able to move or speak. He was hours away from the end of a tough battle with pancreatic cancer.

We talked, and our conversation turned to Christianity and eternal life. Andy's soft, quiet voice became firm when he said, 'I have put my faith in Jesus Christ, my Saviour.'

As I stood next to his bed, tears came to my eyes. He feebly lifted his hand, which I grasped. 'All of us love you so much,' I said. 'I will see you in heaven.'

We can put our complete trust in this promise. In heaven, we will live in eternal peace and joy, praising God.

Because of Jesus' assurance, I do not fear death. I am certain that God will give me the strength to pass from the darkness of this world into the brilliant presence of Christ.

Prayer: *Thank you, God, for sending your Son to show us the way to you. May we glorify you in this world, trusting you to usher us safely into the next, as we pray, 'Father, hallowed be your name, your kingdom come. Give us each day our daily bread. Forgive us our sins, for we also forgive everyone who sins against us. And lead us not into temptation.' (Luke 11:2–4, NIV)*

Thought for the Day: God's promise of resurrection is stronger than the fact of death.

Fred Borchelt (Massachusetts)

PRAYER FOCUS: THOSE WHO ARE GRIEVING

Read the Directions

Read 2 Timothy 3:10–17

Ask in faith, never doubting.

James 1:6 (NRSV)

For his birthday, our young grandson Camden received a toy helicopter with 'some assembly required'. After his grandpa had put it together, the toy would not fly. Then I tried, and his mother gave it a whirl. Still, no flying helicopter.

While each of us worked hard, Camden stood by, watching. Finally, in a calm, matter-of-fact voice he said, 'Maybe we should read the directions.' Hearing his words, we laughed out loud.

At that moment, our daughter assured him, 'When your father gets home, he will put it together for you.' Sure enough, that is just what happened.

What makes us attempt to do something without clear direction? Pride and a false sense of self-reliance may keep us from taking advantage of help that is available to us.

My thoughts went to the many times I have tried to do something on my own without reading God's directions given in the Bible. Rather, desiring to know what God wants me to do, I must seek in faith, not with a doubting mind (see James 1:5–6). When I read God's word and then pray, asking for guidance and wisdom, God gives them freely.

Prayer: *Heavenly Father, giver of all good things, fill our hearts with love for you and for others. Forgive the arrogance that creeps into us. Help us to be pliable and to seek your guidance and direction. Amen*

Thought for the Day: Admitting we need help from God is a sign of strength.

Carolyn Schemahorn (Missouri)

Not Wrong, Just Different

Read Acts 2:1–13

Here there is no Greek or Jew, circumcised or uncircumcised, barbarian, Scythian, slave or free, but Christ is all, and is in all.
Colossians 3:11 (NIV)

I have a friend who is of a different denomination from mine. Because of this difference, she questions my faith, even my salvation. Despite my efforts, she refuses to accept the validity of my Christian faith.

On the day of Pentecost, those who had gathered were from many countries and spoke different languages. But the Holy Spirit touched them all. They all received the Spirit's blessing, and they all praised God in their own languages.

Why do Christians sometimes have such difficulty accepting another person's faith? Each of us is born with our own unique ways of feeling and understanding. These differences don't make us wrong; they simply indicate we are using our God-given gifts to think and reason for ourselves.

God wants us to love each other despite our differences. If we love God honestly, our Christian love can embrace everyone and help us accept that those whose worship practices or theological perspectives differ from ours are still capable of loving God.

Prayer: *O God, you didn't create us all the same. Help us to see and appreciate the beauty in the ways we are different yet still your children. Amen*

Thought for the Day: Our differences can enrich our relationships.

Link2Life: *Befriend someone of another faith or culture.*

Margie J. Harding (Maryland)

Despite the Obstacles

Read Psalm 61:1–5; 62:1–2, 5–8

Whenever you face trials of any kind, consider it nothing but joy, because you know that the testing of your faith produces endurance.
James 1:2–3 (NRSV)

Two or three times a week I take a spiritual walk, taking time to reflect on the will of God for my life. I think about past events and things that are coming up. One day on my walk, I saw some plants that had pushed through the stone wall of a building I was passing. These plants astonished me. The power of life and energy that God put in them had helped them to grow despite obstacles, even through a wall.

In our spiritual life, obstacles and trials can threaten us. Many of us fall into despair when we encounter financial crises, unemployment, conflict and misunderstandings. But the Psalms tell us that God is our refuge and protection. Faith in God helps us to overcome despair.

We can be filled with spiritual strength through prayer, spiritual reflection, Bible reading, fellowship with our brothers and sisters in the faith, fasting and taking Holy Communion in church. When we are filled with God's strength, we mature, becoming strong enough to overcome even the stony obstacles in our path.

Prayer: *O God, we give thanks that you listen to us when we cry out to you. Help us to keep growing in spite of the obstacles in our path, trusting that you will strengthen us. Amen*

Thought for the Day: What obstacles has God helped me to overcome?

Eduard Khegay (Moscow, Russia)

Astounding Grace

Read Matthew 20:1–16
The vineyard owner said, 'Friend, I am doing you no wrong… I choose to give to this last the same as I give to you.'
Matthew 20: 13–14 (NRSV)

My neighbour found the parable of the labourers in the vineyard confusing because it pictures God as unfair, and that cannot be true. I reminded her that the story is a parable, not to be read literally. Besides, the parable does not depict the landowner, who represents God, acting unfairly. The landowner's unconventional fairness teaches us how God treats us. Grace does not fit our usual ideas of justice.

God's divine economy surprises and challenges us. We seek to thrive economically through competition and merit. Generally, we speak of fair wages and assume a person should receive only what he or she earns. In our human economy, grace appears impractical, odd. Yet the parable teaches that God chooses to give us more than we deserve—for that is God's nature.

This idea challenges us as much as it did those who first heard Jesus speak it. We are challenged to appreciate the unconditional nature of God's kindness to everyone and to co-operate in the divine economy of giving more good than people deserve. We do this by approaching our relationships with the grace given through Christ. We who follow him have been entrusted with sharing God's overflowing generosity, lavishing kindness on everyone.

Prayer: *Dear God, help us to be gracious in difficult situations. Let us show your lavish grace in all we do. Amen*

Thought for the Day: If people judged God by my actions, what would they know of grace?

Brian K. Wilcox (Florida)

Thank You!

Read Philippians 4:4–7

Love your enemies, do good, and lend, expecting nothing in return. Your reward will be great, and you will be children of the Most High.
Luke 6:35 (NRSV)

I sent a cheque to a young friend who was struggling to cope on her meagre wages. Because it was a modest amount I didn't expect a lot of excitement, but I hoped for at least a thank you! Hearing nothing, I wondered if she had received the gift. Then, two months later, I bumped into her in town. She offered a casual 'thanks' in answer to my query and said she hadn't had time to deposit the money yet. I felt that my gift was unappreciated, and I wondered whether I would be as open-handed in the future.

Back home I knelt in God's presence, forgiving my friend and confessing my hard feelings. I'm grateful that God is much more gracious than we are. God continues to give to us though we too often forget to return thanks. In 1 Thessalonians 5:18 we read, 'Give thanks in all circumstances; for this is the will of God in Christ Jesus for you.'

God doesn't need our thanks to be happy and content. But our gratitude pleases God; and when we thank our friends and neighbours, we promote their well-being and ours.

Prayer: *Father, help us to remember to say thank you. Forgive us when we hurt others by our thoughtlessness. Amen*

Thought for the Day: Giving thanks honours our generous God.

Brenda Gordon (Aberdeenshire, Scotland)

More than Harmony

Read Acts 2:1–8, 14–21

A great multitude… from every nation, from all tribes and peoples and languages… cried out in a loud voice, saying, 'Salvation belongs to our God… and to the Lamb!'

Revelation 7:9–10 (NRSV)

Polyphony is a musical term. The word literally means 'many sounds'. In polyphony, voices or instruments move independently but work together around a constant central theme. Musician and theologian Jeremy Begbie talks about 'Pentecostal polyphony'. He describes Christ crucified and risen as the constant centre around which the Holy Spirit weaves our diverse lives into a harmonic community called the Body of Christ. Within this community, the Spirit binds our lives together in the love of God.

Here's my version of that: there are no solo performers in the Body of Christ. We can't live singing 'I did it my way' and still claim to be a follower of Jesus. We find out who we are and discover our unique 'song' as our lives are woven into the lives of others in the love of Christ. Dr E. Stanley Jones often said, 'Everyone who belongs to Christ belongs to everyone who belongs to Christ.'

What happened at Pentecost is a living portrait of what God intends for all of creation: many voices, from all nations, races and cultures, singing together in a triumphant song of praise to God (Revelation 7:9–17). In contrast to the world's racism, jingoism, prejudice, hatred and war, each of us is called to help form God's Church into a unified body that sings God's song in all we do.

Prayer: *O God, in all that matters, make us one. Amen*

Thought for the Day: All of us who follow Christ belong to one another.

James A. Harnish (Florida)

Searching for God

Read 1 Kings 19:11–13

The Lord says, 'You will seek me and find me when you seek me with all your heart.'
Jeremiah 29:13 (NIV)

The waves drenched us as the whale-watching boat pitched and tossed, but I was having the time of my life enjoying a boat trip along the Oregon coast. I scanned the surface of the water for a glimpse of the famous grey whale. Would I see a fountain-like spout or a flurry of spray from the slap of a mammoth tail? I didn't know what to expect, but I was sure it would be magnificent.

After an hour's tour, we were taken back to shore. We were on the balcony overlooking the ocean, nursing our disappointment, when a small spray of water announced the presence of a whale. No fountain of water, or leap from the surface confirmed the whale's presence, but the moment thrilled my heart.

I was reminded of Elijah desperately looking for a mighty God in the wind, quaking earth, and fire, only to find God instead in a gentle whisper (1 Kings 19:12). How often do we look for the spectacular, only to discover that God was with us in the ordinary all the time, waiting to be found? We can hear God's voice in a phone call from a friend. We see God's concern in Bible verses that guide us in daily situations. We feel God's touch comforting us in dark nights. We see God revealed quietly in our lives.

Prayer: *Dear God, thank you for all the ways your goodness comes quietly to us. Help us to see them and be grateful. Amen*

Thought for the Day: God's extraordinary goodness comes to us in ordinary days.

Evelyn Beck (Washington)

Not in Vain

Read 1 Corinthians 15:50–58

Unless a grain of wheat falls into the earth and dies, it remains just a single grain; but if it dies, it bears much fruit.
John 12:24 (NRSV)

Lately I have found myself growing discouraged. A marriage ministry that my wife and I have given 15 years of our lives to seems to be coming to an end, despite our best efforts and our belief that this ministry is needed now more than ever. Similarly, a children's choir that we started also seems to be ending.

These disappointments lead to self-doubt and insecurity. We face a constant battle to keep from becoming bitter toward others and toward God. We're doing our part; why isn't God doing more to help us? Even as we struggle, resentment creeps in.

Scripture offers us hope in our discouragement. I have learned that some failures come because we ask God to bless what we are doing, instead of offering ourselves to be used in what God is doing.

Perhaps God is telling us that these former ministries must die in order for other ministries to be born. Paul's letter to the Corinthian church tells us we find hope in Christ's overcoming death, and that as long as our work is in the Lord, it will not be in vain (see 1 Corinthians 15:58).

Prayer: *O God, keep us from bitterness and resentment when our efforts do not yield the results we would like. Help us to trust you, and give us confidence that what we do for you is never done in vain. Amen*

Thought for the Day: Whoever serves Christ will be honoured by God (see John 12:26).

Michael A. Macdonald (North Carolina)

Soaking in God's Word

Read Psalm 77:1–15
Their delight is in the law of the Lord, and on his law they meditate day and night.
Psalm 1:2 (NRSV)

Since I was a child, the Bible has been a part of my day. My parents read it to me when I was very young, and as I grew, they gave me daily devotional guides. My husband and I have begun most of our days reading the Bible and praying together. However, in recent years I have realised that a once-a-day dip into the Bible is not the same as meditating 'day and night'.

My three young sons keep me busy, so time to meditate is hard to find. Because I don't live in my home country, sermons on Sunday are not in a language I understand well. Nevertheless, I must not wait until my children are older to put into practice the discipline of meditating on the words of the Bible. If I don't continue this discipline, my spirit will wilt like a neglected houseplant.

Gradually I have found solutions. Last year I put up a calendar of daily scripture readings. This year I have been posting a chapter from the Bible on the window above the kitchen sink, changing the passage often. Now when I wash up, I can meditate on God's word. As I go about my day, the Bible's truths soak into my heart and revive me moment by moment.

Prayer: *Dear Lord, help us find ways to meditate on your word even when we are busy. Amen*

Thought for the Day: Find a way to think about God's word.

Link2Life: *Copy a favourite Bible verse and put it where you will see it daily.*

Wendy Marshall (Tokyo, Japan)

Prepare and Wait

Read Matthew 6:25–34

'Do not worry about tomorrow, for tomorrow will bring worries of its own.'

Matthew 6:34 (NRSV)

Whenever we talked about worry, my grandmother, a woman of great faith, would say, 'The worst things in my life never happened.' In our reading for today, Jesus talks clearly about worry. He urges his followers to trust in God to meet their needs. Jesus gives examples of the many creatures God has cared for—the birds of the air and the grasses of the field—and promises that our loving God will do no less for us. As I try to apply this passage to my own life, my biggest challenge involves knowing when to act and when to wait for God to act.

A friend helped me understand how to balance the need for personal action and faith in God by describing the acacia tree that grows in the arid plains of central Africa. Acacias endure the droughts of summer, autumn and winter by withering to conserve moisture. But many weeks before the spring rains, the trees start to show green shoots and extend new leaves and new branches to better absorb the as-yet unseen moisture.

I see the acacia as an example of expectant living. We work to get ready before we have proof. And we can live without worry, knowing that a good and gracious God will supply what we need.

Prayer: *Gracious and loving God, give us the wisdom to act in faith even in the face of uncertainty. Amen*

Thought for the Day: Rely on God and live expectantly.

Joseph S Matney (Virginia)

The Real Promised Land

Read Joshua 1:1–9

Through your precepts I get understanding; therefore I hate every false way.
Psalm 119:104 (NRSV)

Dog tired, I stumbled off a cross-country bus and into a cheap hotel long after midnight. I was 18 years old, and all that I owned was in my rucksack. When dawn broke, I gazed out of the window at the Rocky Mountains for the first time. I was sure I had found my promised land, so different from the home I had fled. I was desperate for a new beginning, away from the brokenness of my youth.

Instead, I found the same perils I had left behind—broken relationships, drug abuse and alcoholism. In my misery, I cried out to the Lord. I was led to work for a godly woman who prayed for me and taught me to love the Bible. When I accepted Christ as my Saviour 30 years ago, he began to heal me and gave me hope. In reading the Bible, I learned to live in new ways that brought honour to God and health to my soul.

Sometimes walking away from our problems seems like the answer, but my problems followed me until I learned how to listen to God. I noted how God instructed the wandering Israelites to be strong and courageous, to meditate on the Law and live by its guidance. When I too learned how to obey God by reading the Bible and praying, God gave me the courage to seek help for my addictions and the strength to recover day by day. God's promises are true.

Prayer: *Lord, thank you for the healing that comes when we seek you, trust you and do our best to follow you. Amen*

Thought for the Day: Those who meditate on God's word find the right path.

Rachel Ophoff (Colorado)

Better Than We Deserve?

Read Hebrews 1—2

We see Jesus, who was made a little lower than the angels, now crowned with glory and honour because he suffered death, so that by the grace of God, he might taste death for everyone.

Hebrews 2:9 (NIV)

Jane came to an impoverished, Eastern European village carrying beautifully handcrafted sweaters. In years past, she had visited many of these villagers in their unheated homes. Out of genuine love for the people, she rallied groups at home to donate fine materials and craft the highest quality cold-weather gear. She was bringing her best. When she presented the gifts, a few people glowed with appreciation. But the vast majority took one look and turned up their noses. Jane's gifts, it seemed, were not good enough.

As a witness to this, I struggled with my attitude toward those people until I read Hebrews 2:9, recalling how Christ became a 'little lower than the angels'. He left his seat beside God to come to us with a great gift—salvation. Yet in spite of this, I have often responded to Christ with the attitude that God owes me: God owes me happiness; God owes me a spouse and children; God owes me more than I have already.

But God gives us far more than we deserve. Christ came to us with unconditional love and sacrifice, dying for us. When we understand this reality, we begin to understand grace.

Prayer: *O God, help us to understand that in Jesus Christ you have given us more than we could ever deserve. Help us to share his love with others, as a sign of our gratitude. Amen*

Thought for the Day: Why do we give what we give?

Trudy Chun (Hajdu-Bihar, Hungary)

Shared Tears

Read John 11:32–44
Jesus wept.
John 11:35 (NIV)

When Michael, our 21-year-old son, was killed in a car crash, pain consumed us. Following his death, we were surrounded by family and friends seeking to console us. We knew that their efforts came from the heart and were well-intentioned. Some comments were more helpful than others, but a few were downright hurtful. Hearing 'He's in a better place now' or 'God wanted him to come home' did little to soothe the soul-chilling agony we experienced.

Jesus told his disciples that Lazarus was dead and that he would be raised from the grave. Since Jesus already knew that the story would end in resurrection, why did he weep? I think he was weeping with those who wept, because he loved them, because he was saddened by Mary's anguish.

People who grieve know that crying offers relief and that tears of mourning are a gift of God's grace. We received the most powerful support from men and women who, at a loss for words, simply cried with us. In the face of an awful tragedy, we saw the depth of their love not only for Michael but for us as well. Words have a place, but more powerful is sharing others' pain. When we do that, we embody God's grace for those who mourn.

Prayer: *Heavenly God, help us to break down barriers and to reveal our hearts to those we love. Amen*

Thought for the Day: Weep with those who weep, mourn with those who mourn (see Romans 12:15).

Link2Life: *Send a note to someone who has suffered a recent loss.*

Bill Chadwick (Virginia)

My Old Prayer Notebook

Read Isaiah 55:6–11
*My thoughts are not your thoughts, neither are your ways my ways,
declares the Lord.*
Isaiah 55:8 (NIV)

As I was going through some old belongings, I found a notebook where I had recorded my prayers and requests. I read it with great curiosity. Many of the requests have been granted, but some have not. Of the people I prayed for, some are now dead. Some names seem strange to me.

One of the requests that caught my attention was about a girl who wanted to join her family overseas. God answered that prayer ten years to the day after I started to intercede for her family to be reunited and wrote it in my notebook. I was amazed and thankful for God's way of working.

Sometimes when we pray, we want God to intervene instantly. But sometimes immediate answers don't come. The difficult circumstances in our lives and the times of waiting for God to act can refine our faith, teach us and prepare us for future responsibilities God has for us.

Prayer: *Patient, loving and amazing God, we thank you for your ways of working in our lives. We pray in the name of Jesus Christ. Amen*

Thought for the Day: God answers some prayers immediately, some eventually, and some only in eternity.

Link2Life: *Start a prayer journal or notebook.*

Charlotte Mande Kasongo Lenge (Cape Town, South Africa)

PRAYER FOCUS: GRATITUDE FOR ANSWERED PRAYER

The Joy of the Lord!

Read Job 1

Job said, 'Naked came I out of my mother's womb, and naked shall I return thither: the Lord gave, and the Lord hath taken way; blessed be the name of the Lord!'
Job 1:21 (KJV)

The joy and excitement of my visit to America was suddenly clouded with anxiety. Two of my bags were missing. Overwhelmed, I was becoming a prisoner of worry—something unhealthy for me and also those around me.

Then Job's declaration in the verse above came to my mind. Job had lost all his treasured possessions, and his family was wiped out. I could only guess at the emotional turmoil he must have felt. Yet even after he had endured so much suffering, Job was able still to praise God.

I realised that I too came into this world without anything and will leave without anything. Unlike Job, I had lost only two bags and their contents. My family is well and healthy, and I have enjoyed many blessings from God, all of which I need to give thanks for. This thought gave me the joy, peace of mind and comfort that I needed. Considering the suffering of God's servant Job and Job's response had put my minor suffering into perspective.

Prayer: *Heavenly Father, thank you for your peace and comfort. Teach us to trust and hope in you—both when we have and when we do not have. Amen*

Thought for the Day: Rather than worrying about the little we may have lost, we can thank God for the much we have been given.

Philip Polo (Nairobi, Kenya)

Armchair Outreach

Read Colossians 3:12–17

Let the word of Christ dwell in you richly; teach and admonish one another in all wisdom.
Colossians 3:16 (NRSV)

As a Methodist minister for more than half of the 20th century, whenever I learned that a church member or another friend was in the hospital or in prison, I jumped into my car and made a pastoral call. When a public meeting was called to correct an injustice, I was a participant.

In recent years, an illness that affects my feet and legs has caused me to stop driving. Family members and friends have graciously given me lifts to church, choir practice and community meetings; but my outings have been sharply reduced in number.

I asked myself, 'How can I carry on ministry most effectively in these circumstances?' As I pondered this question, an answer came clearly to my mind: in my new situation, I can minister through intercessory prayer, personal letters and cards, e-mail messages and telephone calls. Every day provides me with opportunities to use one or more of these methods to reach out to people in need. Finding new ways to minister has taken away frustration about my limited mobility and made me grateful for the Christian outreach that is possible from my living-room chair.

Prayer: *Thank you, God, for giving all of us ways to communicate your love and concern to persons in need. In the Spirit of Jesus Christ. Amen*

Thought for the Day: How can I show the love of Christ in my situation?

Link2Life: *Write a note to someone who is confined at home.*

Fred Cloud (Tennessee)

Still There

Read Psalm 27
The Lord's unfailing love and mercy still continue, fresh as the morning, as sure as the sunrise.
Lamentations 3:2–23 (GNB)

Occasionally when I was a child my grandma came to babysit. I can remember once being awake in bed and crying for her. I eventually tiptoed—still crying—into the living-room and found her sitting in front of our cosy coal fire. Surprised to see me so upset, she assured me that she hadn't gone away and would continue watching over me. I went back to bed feeling peaceful and ready to sleep again, knowing that my grandma would never stop loving and caring for me.

Similarly, God never stops loving us, watching over us and working on our behalf. Even so, in the face of illness and injury, disappointment, disaster, bereavement and loneliness, we often struggle to sense God's comforting presence. We long for reassurance that God is still the Lord of our lives and will always love and care for us.

In such times we can remind ourselves that God has promised never to leave us or abandon us (see Hebrews 13:5). Often it is only when we look back at the difficult and hurtful times in our lives that we see God's grace, goodness and faithfulness toward us.

Prayer: *Dear Father, in all our sufferings help us to trust your unchanging love. Through Jesus Christ our Lord. Amen*

Thought for the Day: Though we may change, God doesn't.

Janette Hughson (West Lothian, Scotland)

The Gentle Voice

Read Matthew 11:28–30

Jesus said, 'Take my yoke upon you, and learn from me; for I am gentle..."
Matthew 11:29 (NRSV)

At a county fair I saw an amazing pair of oxen and their young handler at work. This young man had reared the oxen from calves and spent countless hours training them. I sensed a special bond between the handler and his team.

Most teams of oxen are handled by two assistants because the animals become so excited that they start pulling even before they are hitched to the weight. This young handler, however, worked alone. The oxen waited patiently to hear his command; when it came, they made a terrific pull. 'Look at that,' exclaimed the announcer. 'He doesn't have to drive them! He simply asks them to pull!' While other handlers sometimes used whips and harsh words, it took only a few gentle words from this young man for the animals to pull for him.

Christ is like that handler. Seeing the oxen yoked together, I understood more completely what Jesus meant when he said his yoke is easy and his burden is light. Christ is patient with us. He knows that we are capable of much good. Because Christ's voice is gentle, we need not be afraid. When he calls, we can respond out of love, allowing him to guide us. Because Jesus cares for us, our burden is light.

Prayer: *O Lord, thank you for making our burdens light and leading us gently. Amen*

Thought for the Day: Burdens lighten at the sound of Christ's voice.

John W. McKinstry (Massachusetts)

Possible Futures

Read Genesis 22:15–18
I know the plans I have for you, says the Lord, plans for your welfare and not for harm, to give you a future with hope.
Jeremiah 29:11 (NRSV)

I wish I could change parts of my past. Some acts I would not do again. Others that were left undone, I would do. However, time moves forward without mercy. The stories of our lives offer no pauses and no rewinds. Each scene sets the stage for the next.

If we knew only the scene in Abraham's life recounted in the Genesis reading above, we might think this was a man with nothing in his life he would edit. But the Abraham we see in this passage is a person who had been shaped by adversity, doubts and even failures, as well as great acts of faith. Chapters 12—22 in the book of Genesis make this clear. Everything in Abraham's past brought him to Chapter 22's account of faithfulness and blessing. He lived, as we all do, in the unrepeatable present and trusted God who alone owns the future. Thus Abraham becomes for us a living example that 'all things work together for good for those who love God' (Romans 8:28, NRSV).

Each of us is moving toward many possible futures. All of these possibilities have one thing in common for people of Abraham's faith: God who awaits us in the future encompasses all of them. God goes before us just as he went before Abraham.

Prayer: *God of Abraham, help us to live in the present in ways that will bring us where you want us to be in the future. Amen*

Thought for the Day: Our present soon becomes the past that shapes our future.

Daniel Wray (North Carolina)

Linger Longer

Read Isaiah 55:1–3

My soul is satisfied as with a rich feast, and my mouth praises you with joyful lips when I think of you on my bed, and meditate on you in the watches of the night.

Psalm 63:5–6 (NRSV)

I have a friend who lives on Linger Longer Road. Doesn't that name sound inviting? The drive between my home and my friend's takes over an hour. Upon arrival, I feel compelled to stay a while. The address, Linger Longer Road, prompts me to kick off my shoes and relax.

Maybe I should engrave the words 'Linger Longer' on my Bible. On some days, I open the scripture and spend hours reading and savouring a passage. I enjoy God's words as if they were rich food set on a banquet table before me. But I have to admit that on other days, I grab a light snack from scripture and keep walking. I tell the Lord, 'Tomorrow.'

Suppose I invite guests for dinner and fellowship. If they came and asked immediately for a 'doggy bag' to take away with them, I would be insulted. I wonder if God feels the same way about the way we come to the Bible. God wants us to hunger for the love, wisdom and instruction found in the Bible. Do we treat God's word like a fast-food drive-through? Perhaps engraving 'Linger Longer' on the front of our Bibles would entice us to stay a while.

Prayer: *Dear God, lead us to savour your word. Amen*

Thought for the Day: Lingering in God's presence is a feast of love.

Dawn Mooring (Georgia)

Immeasurable Compassion

Read Romans 7:14—8:2

There is... now no condemnation for those who are in Christ Jesus. For the law of the Spirit of life in Christ Jesus has set you free from the law of sin and of death.
Romans 8:1–2 (NRSV)

I still remember the desperate, vulnerable look in Frank's eyes when I opened his door that Sunday. I expected to see my single, quadriplegic friend dressed and ready to accompany me to church; instead, I was confronted with a horrible sight. Frank's motionless body lay rigid and sweaty under his sheet. A full urine bag and an empty water cup with a straw near his mouth meant only one thing—no helper had come to care for him! A care worker's absence had left Frank alone and ignored for hours, incapable of doing even one simple thing for himself. With parched mouth, he had cried out for help. While no human ear heard him, God had! He expressed gratitude and relief as I eagerly rushed to his aid, completely overwhelmed with compassion.

Frank's situation was a vivid reminder of my spiritual dependence on God. I am desperately in need of a saviour to do what I cannot do for myself: cleanse me of sin. Yet God's boundless love and immeasurable compassion toward each of us reach far beyond what I felt for Frank that day. God faithfully delivers us even when others fail.

Prayer: *Thank you, Saviour, for rescuing the needy, those alone and those without help from others. Amen*

Thought for the Day: The love of Christ does for us what we could never do for ourselves.

Jocelyn Davis Rezek (North Carolina)

No Poverty

Read 1 Timothy 6:6–19

Do good... be rich in good works, generous, and ready to share... so that [you] may take hold of the life that really is life.
1 Timothy 6:18–19 (NRSV)

If we were truly to follow God's word, we could make poverty a thing of the past. In the passage above, Paul encouraged Timothy to be content with life and not set his mind on worldly riches, but instead to 'shun [the love of money]; pursue righteousness, godliness, faith, love, endurance, gentleness' (1 Timothy 6:11). He then left a 'commandment' for Timothy—and for us: 'do good... be rich in good works, generous, and ready to share' (1 Timothy 6:18).

Our world has enough resources that no one should be in want; poverty should disappear. But we know that everywhere in the world those who have ample possessions often desire to possess even more, to live above others and to control others' destiny. When we become unwilling to share, we have given up our stewardship and instead revel in our possession of God's world and God's wealth.

True, Paul does not condemn money itself. However, he does speak of the love of money as the root of all evil (see v. 10). The love of money leads to all sorts of selfish acts. But if we become generous and share our riches, we 'store up for [ourselves] the treasure of a good foundation for the future' (v. 19). Only then may we 'take hold of the life' that is really worth living.

Prayer: *Lord, prepare us to listen to your words of challenge—in the Bible and from those you send to us—so that we may share our wealth and ourselves. Amen*

Thought for the Day: We find abundant life when we give ourselves away.

Ike Matshidisho Moloabi (Gauteng, South Africa)

The Journey Home

Read Genesis 32:3–12; 33:1–10

The ransomed of the Lord will return. They will enter Zion with singing; everlasting joy will crown their heads.
Isaiah 51:11 (NIV)

We are all born sinners, and for some reason the ones we hurt the most are usually the ones we love the most. Jacob was no different. He deceived his father and stole from his brother. Jacob was forced to leave home for many years because of his sin. However, there came a time when God called Jacob to return to his family, to go back home and face those he had hurt.

One part of returning home, or going back, is repentance. When we allow sin to live in our hearts, it separates us from the blessings that God wants to give us. Recently, I've been called by God to return home, to repent, to come clean about my past. This process has involved confession to my family about sinful choices I made in my late teens. Like Jacob, I deceived and robbed my family of truth.

Going back home can be very scary. Yet when God directs us to make the journey and we obey, we have the promise that blessings will follow. Those who return to God through his Son, Jesus, are the 'ransomed of the Lord'. We who obey will return and receive everlasting joy. With each step I gain a glimpse of this truth: joy is on the horizon. God is faithful.

Prayer: *Lord, please prepare the way for our return home. Give us enough courage to obey, and prepare those we've hurt to hear the truth. We trust you to guide our steps. Amen*

Thought for the Day: God walks with us on the long road home.

Carol B. Weaver (Texas)

Travelling Standby

Read Isaiah 40:27–31

Neither death, nor life, nor angels, nor rulers, nor things present, nor things to come, nor powers, nor height, nor depth, nor anything else in all creation, will be able to separate us from the love of God in Christ Jesus our Lord.
Romans 8:38–39 (NRSV)

Since my retirement from pastoral ministry I have travelled around the world three times with a volunteer mission organisation. I travel using inexpensive, standby airline tickets available through a family member who is an airline employee. Most of the time I am able to get the flights I want. But sometimes the flights I want are full. In those instances I change to another airline or a different route to reach my destination.

In many ways our lives are like the 'standby' travels I have experienced. It is important to plan ahead for our lives, using our best knowledge to travel faithfully the journey of life. Nevertheless, we encounter disruptions and altered courses. But whether life seems to be running to our schedule or not, we can trust God, who never forsakes us. From Psalm 23 to Romans 8 and many places in between, the Bible speaks to us about God's loving presence with us in both good times and bad.

Prayer: *O God, guide us as we plan and as we travel. Help us always to remember that when the journey is rough, you are close beside us. Amen*

Thought for the Day: Wherever life takes me, the Lord is my shepherd.

Elmer A. Dickson (Florida)

To Keep God's Gifts

Read 1 Timothy 4:11–16

Do not neglect your gift.

1 Timothy 4:14a (NIV)

My wife and I are both in our 80s and have begun to lose our hearing. Our hearing loss has led to some amusing conversations—and to some that were not so amusing, especially when we were in a group of people. So we both decided to have our hearing tested.

We were not surprised to learn that we had both lost a lot of ability to hear. We asked what would happen if we were to muddle along the way we were. The technician explained that hearing is not simply a matter of the ear's capacity to pick up sound waves. Hearing involves the mind learning to interpret different sounds. If poor hearing is ignored, the mind can forget how to interpret particular sounds.

As I thought about the technician's words, I remembered the words of warning from 1 Timothy 4.14: 'Do not neglect your gift.' The gifts of the Spirit are like the gift of hearing. If neglected, they soon drop out of our awareness. We dare not neglect the gifts of the Spirit and the habits of the heart that keep them fresh in our lives: prayer, studying the Bible, worshipping with the community of faith. These help us to appreciate the wonder of our daily walk in faith and to pay attention to God.

Prayer: *Gracious God, keep our hearts tuned to the gifts you have given. Amen*

Thought for the Day: How can I more fully use my spiritual gifts?

Link2Life: *Take a spiritual gifts inventory.*

David Knecht (North Dakota)

Without Wavering

Read Hebrews 11:1–7

Faith is being sure of what we hope for and certain of what we do not see.

Hebrews 11:1 (NIV)

I grew up and live in a house with wide rooms and big, bright windows. In winter when temperatures are low, moisture on the windows freezes, creating beautiful icy flowers that seem to be painted by a master painter. When my children were young, we wondered at these lovely pictures and delighted in them.

But even when a cold winter brings few delights, we have hope that spring is coming. The snow melts and ice flowers give way to small and beautiful spring flowers in the garden. The sun's rays warm our hearts.

In all seasons God can refresh our spirit through the beauty of creation. It can show us the Creator's loving presence—not only in nature but in every area of life. God renews our hope again and again. Therefore, we can join with the writer of Hebrews in proclaiming, 'Let us hold fast to the confession of our hope without wavering, for he who has promised is faithful' (Hebrews 10:23, NRSV).

Prayer: *God, help us hold fast to our hope in you. As Jesus taught us, we pray, 'Our Father in heaven, hallowed be your name, your kingdom come, your will be done on earth as it is in heaven. Give us today our daily bread. Forgive us our debts, as we also have forgiven our debtors. And lead us not into temptation, but deliver us from the evil one.' (Matthew 6:9–13, NIV)*

Thought for the Day: God constantly renews our hope.

Link2Life: *Each hour this day, look for one sign of hope.*

Mariam Altunian (Shumen, Bulgaria)

PRAYER FOCUS: THOSE WHOSE TRUST IN GOD WAVERS

A Feast Every Day

Read Psalm 130

O Israel, put your hope in the Lord, for with the Lord is unfailing love and… full redemption.
Psalm 130:7 (NIV)

It was a hot day, and my husband and I drove to a nearby restaurant for the air conditioning as much as for the food. The chips tasted so good that we quickly finished our portions. 'Would you like more?' the waiter asked. When he saw that we were hesitating, he said, 'I will bring you more. There is always plenty.'

That is similar to the way God deals with us. God doesn't offer just a little redemption, doesn't forgive a few of our sins. God offers full redemption, in abundance. It's like a feast every day, and the main dish on the menu is forgiveness.

Because God offers more than enough redemption for me, I can invite more people to the table. My job is to make sure that the abundance doesn't go to waste. I need to go to everyone, even to my colleagues and the people who live next door, to share the news of this abundant pardon with them. I think I will start today by asking my neighbour how I can pray for her. I've invited her to church and I've baked a cake for her, but I've never actually talked to her about the abundant redemption God offers. I will begin today. God's feast is always ready.

Prayer: *Dear God, thank you for the feast of love you provide. Help me remember to invite those around me to your table. Amen*

Thought for the Day: Am I offering God's redemption to the people I know?

Christie Jenkins (California)

High-Rise Perspective

Read Ephesians 3:14–21

To [God] who is able to do immeasurably more than all we ask or imagine, according to his power that is at work within us, to him be glory in the church and in Christ Jesus throughout all generations.
Ephesians 3:20–21 (NIV)

Recently I had the opportunity to go to the top floor of the second-tallest building in the city where I live. I really didn't think much about it before going. However, once I got to the top of the building and looked out of the window, my whole perspective on the city changed. At street level objects and sounds are big, loud and fast; but from the top of a high-rise building, they seem much smaller, quieter and more peaceful. I was amazed at how different the entire city appeared when I was looking at it from a higher vantage point.

A similar thing happens when we look at human life. The troubles and trials around us can seem overwhelming from our viewpoint, but as we grow closer to God and focus more on God's kingdom, we begin to see our world from a different perspective. We can see that God is much larger than any of the problems we face, and we begin to understand that God is indeed 'able to do immeasurably more than all we ask or imagine, according to his power that is at work within us'.

Prayer: *Lord, help us to see our world the way you see it. When troubles arise, help us to remember that you are greater than anything that may happen to us. Amen*

Thought for the Day: Knowing God changes the way we see the world.

Link2Life: *Examine a map/photo and ponder God's perspective.*

Mike Barclay (Indiana)

Follow by Going

Read Matthew 4:18–22
'Come, follow me,' Jesus said.
Matthew 4:19 (NIV)

For Peter, Andrew, James and John the call was clear. Jesus invited them to leave what they were doing to follow him. And they did! Later Jesus set them to work, saying, 'The harvest is plentiful, but the workers are few' (Luke 10:2).

That was then; but what about today? I want to follow Jesus, but he's not walking down the busy streets of my town. Or is he? While those early disciples could follow in Jesus' earthly footsteps, we have the Holy Spirit who helps us to know Christ's voice. As individuals, we are called to serve God in many different places. One may follow Jesus to a foreign land; another may follow him into a schoolroom. Some may follow him to the business world, while others may serve in public office or as homemakers, taxi drivers or police officers.

The field that Jesus talked about is all around us. Not only is it across the ocean; it is in the house next door, the desk across from ours at work, the playground where our children play. In these places we follow Jesus, sharing his love so that other people can respond to his voice and follow him, too.

Prayer: *Lord Jesus, teach us to walk with you today. Make us willing to go wherever you lead us. Amen*

Thought for the Day: No matter where we work, we can work for God.

Jill Woodward (Georgia)

Guided by Faith

Read Romans 8:28–39

If we hope for what we do not see, we wait for it with patience.
Romans 8:25 (NRSV)

When the Zapatista movement in Mexico was at its peak, I was assigned to reconnaissance flights over the occupied territory held by this group. On one mission, all was well until a sudden change in weather dropped visibility to zero and we were forced to navigate using the instrument panel. My first thought was 'Why me, Lord?'

Protocol under these conditions is to remain calm and trust the instrument panel with its directional indicator, altitude indicator, and altimeter. In this scenario, failure to pay attention to the situation at hand can result in spatial disorientation—not knowing which way is up.

Many drastic circumstances can also cause us to lose our bearings—loss of employment, a threatening legal matter, the death of a loved one. In difficult moments, when we ask 'Why me?' God instructs us to remain faithful and strong. When life's challenges strain our faith, we can hold fast to our directional indicator, the Bible, which will show us the way. God's word helps us discover how to navigate through life's challenges. Because of this, we can remain strong in the face of adversity, sustained by faith.

Prayer: *God of the universe, stand by us in the hour of our need so that adversity will not overwhelm us. Grant that we remain strong and faithful. Amen*

Thought for the Day: When the weather gets rough, we can trust God to guide us.

Gilberto de la Rosa Rodriguez (Leon, Mexico)

Follow Jesus

Read Psalm 71:5–8

Jesus told his disciples, 'If any want to become my followers, let them deny themselves and take up their cross and follow me.'
Matthew 16:24 (NRSV)

Oh, how I wish the words of this passage in Psalm 71 described me. As a child, I accepted as fact that Jesus died on a cross and was raised back to life. Although I thought I was a Christian, following Jesus was not the focus of my life. I was. My hopes, prayers, and thoughts generally revolved around me and my needs. My confidence was in myself.

Years later, I came to understand that being a Christian means submitting myself to Christ Jesus as my Lord, following him, and submitting to his plans for me. It means resting in the love and the peace he gives. It means so much more than this and so much more than I understood as a child.

Whether we grew up loving Christ Jesus and relying on him every day, or rarely thinking of him, we can't change the past. Tomorrow is not here, but we have this moment. Jesus said, 'Follow me.' That we can do. Right now. This moment.

Prayer: *Lord Jesus, we submit our desires, our plans and our lives to you. Help us, Lord, to follow you. Amen*

Thought for the Day: Only what's done for Christ will last.

Star Ferdinand (Texas)

The Present

Read Luke 12:22–32

'Do not worry about your life, what you will eat, or about your body, what you will wear. For life is more than food, and the body more than clothing.'

Luke 12:22–23 (NRSV)

Watching my son open presents on his sixth birthday, I thought back to the day of his birth. When the doctor told us that Justice had Down's syndrome, I became consumed with worry about the future. I imagined weekly doctor's visits about medical problems and other challenges that I was sure I would have to deal with. On that birthday, as I watched Justice open presents, I suddenly realised that he has brought more joy into my life than I ever could have imagined. Instead of hardship and pain, our son has brought into our family peace, love and joy. The things I had worried about when he was born never came to pass. He is healthy, happy and full of life. I suddenly realised that Justice has given me far more than worry and a fear of the future.

As I watched my son, joy filled my heart. I realised that God had also given *me* a present. My gift was not only our child, but also awareness that life is to be lived in the present. Justice is a gift, and he teaches me to live each day as it comes.

Prayer: *Heavenly Father, thank you for giving us this moment. Please help us live in the present and to trust you more every day. Amen*

Thought for the Day: Live each day fully and eagerly, as the gift from God that it is.

Link2Life: *Send a copy of this to the parents of a special-needs child, or list your worries and put the list in your Bible, committing it to God.*

Jay Wollenburg (Ohio)

Preparing for—?

Read Lamentations 3:21–25
No eye has seen, nor ear heard, nor the human heart conceived, what God has prepared for those who love him.
1 Corinthians 2:9 (NRSV)

My favourite deciduous tree was looking tired and untended. Halfway through autumn, the magnolia was losing its leaves. Those that had not yet fallen hung limply, looking dejected. Leaves that had been a vibrant green just a week or two earlier had turned pale tan; most of the colour had leached out of them.

A few days later, my magnolia tree looked quite different. The upper limbs, devoid of leaves, showed newly formed buds, poised and waiting for the opportunity to bloom. Instead of a tree that appeared tired and dull, it suggested to me new life and new hope. Although winter had not yet arrived, this tree was already preparing itself for the wonders of spring.

At times we too seem to be limply hanging around, waiting for something to happen. At these times God is preparing us for the next season or the next change we are to undergo. Sometimes we are unaware of the imperceptible changes God is busily achieving within us. Then, at the right moment, we find ourselves in a new situation. We marvel that God has been at work, preparing us for something we could not have imagined or prepared ourselves for.

Prayer: *Dear God, we thank you for your renewing spirit. Amen*

Thought for the Day: Watch out; God is always up to something.

Meg Mangan (New South Wales, Australia)

Dad's Gift

Read James 2:14–26
Do not forget to do good and to share with others, for with such sacrifices God is pleased.
Hebrews 13:16 (NIV)

I share a birthday with my dad. He calls me 'the best gift ever', but I am certain that he has given me a greater gift.

On a birthday years ago, I had no present for my dad. I started to cry; and Dad comforted me, explaining that material gifts are not the most important ones. He told me that being a good person and doing what is right would be my greatest gift to him.

From that moment, I committed to do at least one act of kindness each day. Since then, my life has been enriched. While I miss a day on occasion, most days I revel in the gift of giving. Whether I made a meal for a housebound person, wrote a letter of appreciation, cleared snow from a colleague's car, or mowed a neighbour's lawn, I have been blessed.

By keeping that birthday pledge, I have grown closer to God, found opportunities to tell the good news, and tried to model Christian behaviour. And over the years, friends, family members, colleagues and neighbours have learned of my practice of daily kindness and adopted this pattern of giving themselves. While most of my childhood toys are gone, the pledge I made to my dad has endured the storms of my life. I truly received the greater gift because of his wisdom.

Prayer: *Thank you, God, for the wisdom of our elders, for your selfless acts of love, and for opportunities to give with a cheerful heart. Amen*

Thought for the Day: What can I do to make another person's day a little brighter?

Kerry Riddle (New York)

PRAYER FOCUS: TO GIVE UNSELFISHLY OF OURSELVES

Impossible Task?

Read Nehemiah 1:1–11; 6:15–16

David sang to God, 'With your help I can advance against a troop; with my God I can scale a wall.'
2 Samuel 22:30 (NIV)

Although I felt led by God to begin a new project, I was facing an impossible task. Getting started has never been my problem; I tend to begin with enthusiasm and faith. Finishing is the difficult part for me. As I pondered this new project for weeks, the book of Nehemiah kept popping into my mind.

Nehemiah was a cup bearer to King Artexexes of Persia. With the king's permission, Nehemiah began what must have seemed like an impossible task—rebuilding the crumbled walls around Jerusalem. The walls had lain in ruins for 100 years, and must have seemed beyond repair. Undaunted, Nehemiah studied the task, quietly made his plans, organised the people, and rebuilt the walls in 52 days, despite facing many obstacles.

Think about it: 52 days fraught with troubles, with no modern machines, no paid workers, nothing but God's help. But God's help is all that really mattered. It isn't the magnitude of the task; it's the magnitude of our God that counts most.

We can ask ourselves, 'What impossible task am I facing today? What walls do I have to scale?' God helped Nehemiah, and God wants to help us too. When God ordains a project, God provides help from beginning to end.

Prayer: *Holy God, grant us faith to believe and perseverance to hold on to your promise of help. Amen*

Thought for the Day: With God's help we can scale a wall, build one, or tear one down.

Lana Vannarsdall (Kentucky)

Knowing God

Read Psalm 91:1–2

Jesus said, 'Surely I am with you always, to the very end of the age.'
Matthew 28:20 (NIV)

All my life I have heard about God, but it is one thing to know about God and another to live in relationship with God. Through the years, I have grown in my faith slowly. Two-and-a-half years ago, I faced the challenge that required me to act on my faith.

When my husband of over 50 years passed away, I was devastated. I didn't know what to do. Our children had grown up, and it had been just the two of us for over 30 years. Suddenly I was all alone.

In my loneliness and grief, God led me to look back over my life. I saw that many times God had been there, supporting and strengthening me, though I had not recognised God's presence at the time. I recalled Jesus' words, 'I will never leave you nor forsake you' (Joshua 1:5).

I can truly say that God is the only one on whom we can depend. When everyone leaves, God is with us. Though we go through hard times, we can rest assured that God is with us. Even our Lord Jesus felt abandoned on the cross; he knows how we feel and he is our great comforter. Thanks be to God!

Prayer: *Thank you, God, for your loving care that will never end. Thank you for the promise that you will never leave us. Amen*

Thought for the Day: In our loneliest moments, God reaches out to us.

Janet White (Victoria, Australia)

Blooming Christians

Read Matthew 25:14–29

Encourage one another and build each other up... warn those who are idle, encourage the timid, help the weak, be patient with everyone... always try to be kind to each other and to everyone else.
1 Thessalonians 5:11, 14, 15 (NIV)

Each spring a rhododendron bush in my garden is covered in frilly pink flowers. Not all the buds open at the same time, however. For a while, fully unfurled and half-opened blossoms share space with tight, green buds that give no hint of opening. But I know that warmed by sun, nourished by soil, and refreshed by rain, those green buds will bloom in due course.

Christians also bloom at different times. Some serve visibly and eagerly in the church as ministers, teachers and leaders or with the hungry and homeless in the community. Others, like half-opened flowers, reluctantly agree to help on committees. Then there are those whose growth is less obvious to us. Like unopened buds, they need the warmth of fellowship, the nourishment of God's word and the refreshment of love in order to bloom.

We cannot hurry the spiritual growth of others any more than I can force my rhododendron to bloom. But we may provide a climate for growth by inviting people into our homes, by discussing current issues from a biblical viewpoint, and by letting the love of God flow through us to meet their needs.

Prayer: *O God, help us to bloom as faithful disciples in the world around us. Amen*

Thought for the Day: How am I nurturing others in the faith?

Shirley Brosius (Pennsylvania)

People Will Sing

Read Isaiah 12:1–6

The Lord gives me power and strength; he is my Saviour.
Isaiah 12:2 (GNB)

I listened with delight as my young grandson sang to me. His happy face mirrored what his words expressed. Often, singing enables us to express longings, hopes and dreams that cannot be shared by mere spoken or written language.

The Bible reading for today contains the prophecy that God's people will suffer judgment for their sins and unfaithfulness. But Isaiah also states, 'A day is coming when people will sing' (12:1) in the midst of their suffering. Throughout chapter 12, Isaiah chooses the word 'sing' to describe the exiles' response to God's promise that they would return to their land.

We all deal with losses and disappointments; but we can remain faithful and hopeful because we know that our labour in the Lord is not in vain (see 1 Corinthians 15:58) and that God gives us the power and the strength to face life's obstacles. And in the midst of our sadness, suffering and emptiness, we have Isaiah's promise that a day is coming when we will be able to sing again.

Prayer: *Thank you, Father, for the hope that your words bring us. We pray as Jesus taught us, saying, 'Our Father which art in heaven, Hallowed be thy name. Thy kingdom come. Thy will be done, as in heaven, so in earth. Give us day by day our daily bread. And forgive us our sins; for we also forgive every one that is indebted to us. And lead us not into temptation; but deliver us from evil.' (Luke 11:2–4, KJV)*

Thought for the Day: We will sing again.

Sherry Brooks Martin (South Carolina)

To Honour God

Read John 15:9–17

Jesus said, 'If you obey my commands, you will remain in my love, just as I have obeyed my Father's commands and remain in his love.'
John 15:10 (NIV)

As an assistant principal at an elementary school, I often talk with children about their behaviour. One day, six-year-old Tommy arrived at my office with a note from his teacher. The note said that Tommy had refused to complete his class assignment and thrown a tantrum in front of the other students.

'I don't want to do any work,' Tommy said as he stood before me, his arms folded across his chest. After he had dried his tears, I reminded him that as a pupil at the school, one of his jobs was to follow the rules. He could not do what he wanted to do but rather needed to obey his teacher's instructions and make better choices about his behaviour.

Each day we all make decisions. God has given us a free will, and we decide whether we are going to honour God by living as the Bible directs, loving and serving others, or rebel against God by doing only what we want to do. God wants to guide us toward wise choices about how we live. With open and loving arms, God waits for us to trust and obey.

Prayer: *Dear God, may all that we do today please you. Amen*

Thought for the Day: We honour God by obeying him.

Link2Life: *Make a list of your recent decisions. In which of them did you consult God for direction?*

James C. Hendrix (Indiana)

At the Bus Stop

Read 1 Samuel 16:1, 6–12

The Lord does not see as mortals see; they look on the outward appearance, but the Lord looks on the heart.
1 Samuel 16:7 (NRSV)

I arrived at the bus stop with my three-year-old son and looked at the other commuters already there. One woman stood out because of her stern face, seemingly set in permanent lines of unyielding harshness. My son, however, not given to rash judgments, approached the bench where she was sitting, looked into her eyes, and engaged her in conversation. 'Hello. What's your name?' he asked, placing a gentle hand on her knee. Before my eyes, her stern face dissolved and her eyes softened as she responded to the irresistible charm of a friendly child.

His actions and her response caused me to think about the way we respond to others. How often do we miss out on rich relationships because we do not make an effort to get to know people we have judged to be not worth the effort?

Jesus touched people whom others shunned. He wants us to be his hands, his heart and his voice to those who may seem unapproachable or unattractive. Some people will respond instantly, as the woman at the bus stop did. Others may require nurture over time. But each one is worth the effort. After all, God has worked on us over time—and is still doing it!

Prayer: *Lord, help us to see others through your eyes of love. Amen*

Thought for the Day: A tender word can call forth unexpected warmth.

Link2Life: *Reach out to someone near you who seems unfriendly.*

Colette Williams (South Australia, Australia)

PRAYER FOCUS: SOMEONE I HAVE JUDGED BY APPEARANCE

Help for Heavy Burdens

Read 2 Chronicles 32:1–8

Be strong and of good courage. Do not be afraid or dismayed… for there is one greater with us than with [the king of Assyria]. With him is an arm of flesh; but with us is the Lord our God.

2 Chronicles 32:7–8 (NRSV)

Hezekiah's many faithful acts are recorded in the Bible. He learned that in every circumstance there was his part and there was God's part. Such was the case as he encountered Sennacherib, the king of Assyria, whose intent was to capture Jerusalem. King Hezekiah did all he could to prevent an Assyrian victory. He built walls, made weapons and shields, organised the people and stopped the flow of water to the springs from which the enemy drank. Having done his part, Hezekiah called on God to do the rest of what was needed.

Occasionally, we need to be reminded that a portion of life's task is ours to do. But we should also remember that there are times when life's burdens can become overwhelming. Crushed, we find we cannot manage life's demands by ourselves. That's when it's time to turn more fully to God. We do our part, of course; but when adversity gets beyond us, we can turn to the Lord for help. Our faithfulness will be rewarded as God gives us strength sufficient for our tasks.

Prayer: *Helper of the helpless, empower us to trust you more. Make us aware of your hand holding ours. Let us be assured that when all other helpers fail, you remain present. Amen*

Thought for the Day: Life is meant to be a partnership between us and God.

William L. Dike (Florida)

PRAYER FOCUS: SOMEONE FEELING OVERWHELMED

A Place to Call Home

Read Psalm 23

Jesus said, 'In my Father's house are many rooms; if it were not so, I would have told you. I am going there to prepare a place for you.'
John 14:2 (NIV)

'I want to go home,' my elderly aunt said with tears in her voice. I wished I could lessen her pain. The last time I'd visited her she had prepared a family meal at the home where she had lived for over 50 years. Now my mum and I had come to see her in a nursing home. In the space of three years, her world had changed forever. Her husband had died, her health was deteriorating, and her only child was unable to care for her.

As we got ready to leave, Aunt Elizabeth (not her real name) sadly uttered, 'No.' Mum hugged her and prayed, 'Jesus, thank you that you're here with Aunt Elizabeth. Help her to know that you'll never leave her, and that you're preparing a new home for her in heaven.' As my aunt walked with us to the exit, I felt as if I was abandoning her to loneliness in a situation she was powerless to change. 'How would I cope in her situation?' I wondered. As we turned away, waving goodbye, Mum began to weep. Not long after our visit, Aunt Elizabeth went to see her Saviour face to face.

We all want and need a place to call home. Changes come into all our lives, maybe through illness, loss of job or family, or moving. But Christ promises to prepare a place for us in heaven—a permanent home with him.

Prayer: *Lord Jesus, thank you for the hope we have because of our trust in you and because of your loving provision for us. Amen*

Thought for the Day: Even when our earthly home is gone, we have a place with God.

Joy E. Miller (Virginia)

Perched on the Word

Read Luke 6:46–49
Your word, O Lord, is eternal; it stands firm in the heavens.
Psalm 119:89 (NIV)

My wife and I are fortunate to be able to spend part of the year on a little island off the coast of Florida. The weather changes constantly. As we awoke this morning, a storm was approaching. We watched in awe as the strength of the wind increased. Staring out over the water, we caught sight of a flock of ibises heading for shore and safety. Their flight was disrupted by frequent, strong gusts of wind; but after much struggle, they reached the shore and settled on the bare limbs of some mangrove trees. Tired as the birds were, the wind was unable to dislodge them from their perch.

Those birds remind me that if we live by God's word, nothing can dislodge us from our perch in life. In our ever-changing world, God's message, found in the word of scripture, will be stable for all time.

Do you believe that God exists? Do you believe God will act in your life?

Prayer: *God, we praise and thank you for the wonders of your creation, from the smallest creatures to the highest mountains to the deepest seas. May we continue to live by your word as we grow closer to you. We ask you to guide us through the storms of life until we come home to you for all eternity. Amen*

Thought for the Day: The word of the Lord is our stability.

Richmond de P. Talbot, Jr. (Florida)

Spiritual Amnesia

Read Psalm 145:1–7

In your hearts set apart Christ as Lord. Always be prepared to give an answer to everyone who asks you to give the reason for the hope that you have. But do this with gentleness and respect, keeping a clear conscience, so that those who speak maliciously against your good behaviour in Christ may be ashamed of their slander.
1 Peter 3:15 (NIV)

Recently I was challenged to write down all the times God has intervened in my life, including answers to prayers or help that came undeniably from God. I spent days mulling over my past and God's involvement in my life, but I struggled to recall specific examples. Stunned by my spiritual amnesia, I realised I was no better than the Israelites who forgot all that the Lord had done for them. Nevertheless, the number of entries I eventually recorded created awareness of God's activity throughout my life.

When we ask for help in remembering, God helps us recall the interventions we have witnessed. God wants us not only to remember but to tell others how we have seen God work. When we are alert, it's amazing how often opportunities to tell others about them present themselves. Talking about God's help, healing and peace reminds us how loving and powerful God is. We encourage others and glorify God when we make known what God has done for us. We also become more mindful of and thankful for our own blessings.

So, what has God done for you? Do you remember?

Prayer: *O God, help us to encourage others by sharing our stories of your love and power in our lives. Amen*

Thought for the Day: Telling others how God has worked in our life can prevent spiritual amnesia.

Cindy Rooy (Tennessee)

What Do You See?

Floating in a small bowl of water in my refrigerator are seven four-leaf clovers. That's right—seven. I have been collecting these for several weeks since a young friend said to me, 'I really, really want to see a real four-leaf clover. Are they hard to find?'

Remembering that conversation, a few days later I paused to look more closely than usual at a patch of clover. I saw rising slightly above the many three-leaf clovers one with four leaves. Of course I picked it for my friend. Since then, I have made it a point to look at patches of clover when I walk my dog. After seeing the unusual clover I found, my young friend began looking for them, too. So far she has found more than a dozen in her garden— sometimes several in an afternoon.

Do our experiences prove that we grow more four-leaf clovers where I live than in most places? I don't think so. We find them because we look carefully at what is before us. We don't assume that all the sprigs are the same and have only three leaves. And because our eyes are open, we see what is there.

It occurred to me that we sometimes look at people—especially people we know well—the way I used to look at clover patches, not really seeing them at all. We operate on our idea of who they are and do not actually look at them as they are today, this moment. They're just one among many, all alike, nothing special—like a patch of clover. We know what's there, so we don't have to look.

What if we decided to look at people differently? What if we approached those around us in their 'holy uniqueness', assuming that they are special—because they are? What if we made it a pattern to remember why we value them?

I heard a story about an interview with a couple who had been married for more than 50 years. The interviewer asked the wife,

'What is the secret to your long marriage?'

'Well, when we married, I decided that I would overlook ten things about my husband because I love him, because he's a good man. I wouldn't let these things bother me. I wouldn't get upset by them.'

'And what are those ten things?'

'Oh, I don't actually have a list. But every time he did something that just drove me crazy, I'd say to myself, "That's one of the ten."'

That woman had found a useful strategy. The people we are closest to all have good traits. But sometimes we don't see them for the best of who they are. In fact, we may find ourselves focusing mainly on traits that annoy us. The Bible holds up another standard: 'Whatever is true, whatever is honourable, whatever is just, whatever is pure, whatever is pleasing, whatever is commendable… think about these things' (Philippians 4:8, NRSV).

Our familiarity with those closest to us can blind us to the work God is doing in them or may want to do through them. This is nothing new. When Jesus went to his hometown to preach, he was unable to do many miracles there. He could only 'heal a few sick' people. Seeing this, he commented, 'Prophets are not without honour, except in their hometown, and among their own kin' (Mark 6:4, NRSV). Our blindness to God's presence in those around us may limit or block what they do or attempt to do for God, as happened with Jesus.

Every interaction is unique. As ordinary as our conversations may be, Christ is present in them—and so they are blessed in their ordinariness. We will never live this moment, with this person, again. Whether we are laughing together at a film, sweating as we clean the garage or dig the garden, weeping at the bedside of someone we love or looking for four-leaf clovers, this moment is unrepeatable. This person is irreplaceable. This relationship is unique—and holy in its uniqueness.

God does not usually call to us through burning bushes (see Exodus 3), transforming the ordinary in ways so spectacular that we cannot miss what is happening. But when we pay attention, God does call to us continually, through ordinary situations. The people we see each day are messengers and agents of what God wants to tell us, show us, give us, day in, day out. Will we listen? Will we see?

You may want to read again the meditations for May 1, 6, 10, 14, 16, 19, 21, 23, and 24; June 2, 9, 11, 13, 15, 18, 20, 23 and 26; and July 4 and 22 before answering the questions below.

Questions for Reflection:

1. When has some small behaviour caused you to lose sight of someone's basic goodness? How might you remind yourself to concentrate instead on the way the people close to you are gifts in your life?

2. Where have you recently seen God in some ordinary situation? What opened your eyes to God's presence?

3. What spiritual practices can help us to look more closely and lovingly at those around us?

4. Are you naturally a person who looks at the positive, who sees the best in others, or naturally someone who tends to be more analytical or critical? How can we change this part of our behaviour? Should we?

5. How have past encounters with critical people affected you? Does criticism help people grow toward what God wants for each of us?

6. Think of two or three people you know well and describe the 'holy uniqueness' you see in them. How can you help them to see their giftedness and value?

Mary Lou Redding

Remembering to Breathe

Read Psalm 63:1–8

O God, you are my God, earnestly I seek you; my soul thirsts for you, my body longs for you, in a dry and weary land where there is no water.
Psalm 63:1 (NIV)

I have spent my adult life caring for severely premature babies. One of their common problems is forgetting to breathe, requiring a touch by a nurse to remind them to resume normal respiration. They are surrounded by life-giving air but are at risk of dying because their immature brain fails to send the signal to breathe.

I think my spiritual life is sometimes like that. I am surrounded by the presence of God, but my immaturity causes me not to breathe spiritually. I skip reading my Bible, ignore my need for quiet time, shy away from talking to God. All these are necessary for breathing in the Holy Spirit and for cleansing my soul of the toxic elements of life that accumulate within all of us.

When I become 'air hungry', depressed and seemingly without hope, the hand of God touches me, much like a nurse who cares for the premature infant. Then I realise that I feel empty because I have forgotten the most important of daily activities—breathing in the life of God's Holy Spirit. When I realise I am not 'breathing' regularly, I return to my quiet time and am renewed by God's loving presence.

Prayer: *Dear Lord, thank you for your touch that reawakens our desire to breathe in your saving life. Amen*

Thought for the Day: Time with God is as necessary as breathing.

Keith J. Peevy (Alabama)

PRAYER FOCUS: PREMATURE INFANTS AND THEIR PARENTS

A Generous God

Read Matthew 20:1–16
The landowner said, 'Are you jealous because I am generous?'
Matthew 20:15 (GNB)

Since I was a young child, I've been a Christian—and I fully intend to serve God until the day I die. Because of this, the people I've always identified with most in the parable of the vineyard workers are those who were hired early in the day. They were the ones who started the job early and did their best to get the job done. They were hard-working, diligent and responsible, and after doing a full day of work they deserved their pay. I can understand why they would get upset if someone else started work as the day ended and got paid the same wage as for a full day of work. If I were in their position, I would be jealous too when the boss was generous.

That we find it so easy to identify with these workers is a main point of the parable, really. Nothing that we can do will earn us the right to spend eternity in heaven. It does not matter if we follow God for our entire lives or just in our last days, the only way we can enter heaven is through accepting the gift of salvation won for us on the cross by Christ Jesus. The God we serve is generous, no matter when we come to repentance.

Prayer: *God of all the world, we praise you for your boundless, generous love. In Jesus' name we pray. Amen*

Thought for the Day: Whether we come early or come late, we are precious to God.

Joanna Ronalds (Victoria, Australia)

PRAYER FOCUS: THOSE TRYING TO EARN GOD'S LOVE AND APPROVAL

God at Work!

Read Psalm 139:1–24

He who began a good work in you will carry it on to completion until the day of Christ Jesus.

Philippians 1:6 (NIV)

I took a visiting overseas pastor to Wells Cathedral, one of the jewels of our English Christian heritage. It reflects the craftsman-ship of centuries of stonemasons, builders, workers of stained glass, wood-turners, carpenters and painters. Each person's artistry was designed to raise the eye to God, to lift thoughts beyond our earthly perception and understanding to God's kingdom and glory. 'So,' asked my visitor, 'how long did it take them to build this—ten years?' We laughed as I pointed out an information board and read 'around 200 years'!

How often others have a different perception of our achieve-ments than we have known. What we have been struggling to over-come for a lifetime, others may not even notice. Not so with God. He knows where we are coming from. He sees each step of trust we take and holds our hand as we journey. We may have issues of forgiveness, or the healing from past trauma, or addictions, or loss, ill health or new beginnings. We may be rebuilding our lives after disaster or destruction. God's love still has a purpose for us, and he never gives up on his handiwork.

Prayer: *Thank you, Father, that you never give up on me, never abandon me, but are willing to bring your good work in me to completion. Amen*

Thought for the Day: 'Like clay in the hand of the potter, so are you in my hand' (Jeremiah 18:6).

Hilary Allen, (Somerset, England)

The Good Shepherd

Read John 10:7–16

Jesus said, 'There are other sheep which belong to me that are not in this sheep pen. I must bring them, too.'

John 10:16 (GNB)

Whenever I hear or read John 10:7–16, I am comforted. In this passage Jesus assures us of his care for his sheep and adds that his chosen ones are free to come and go from his enclosure to find pasture. He also affirms that before his work is complete, he will gather in more sheep.

The scripture leads me to believe that the others Jesus calls may not be people I would choose to be with. I may dismiss them as not belonging to Jesus' flock because their ways of practising their faith are different from mine.

However, the Bible offers many examples of God calling people we probably would not choose: Moses killed a man. Samuel was only a boy. Rahab was a prostitute. The woman at the well was a social outcast. Peter denied even knowing Jesus, and Paul helped to hunt down Jesus' followers.

Anyone I meet may well be among the 'other sheep' Christ has chosen to bring into the fold. Perhaps when meeting people who are not yet Christians, I should consider that they are on their way to Jesus, that they will soon be part of the flock too.

Prayer: *God, help us to see people as Jesus saw them and to offer love, respect and acceptance for who they are rather than for who we would like them to be. Amen*

Thought for the Day: Love others as you find them, not as you wish they were.

Betty Madill (Aberdeenshire, Scotland)

Relying on Grace

Read Romans 8:18–31

Though you search for your enemies, you will not find them. Those who wage war against you will be as nothing at all.
Isaiah 41:12 (NIV)

'Why is this happening again? I thought we had beaten this! What did we do wrong? It's just so unfair!' my wife said. My tears mixed with hers as we heard the oncologist say that the cancer had returned. We thought it was cured two years ago, but now more chemotherapy lay ahead.

Our faith, especially our reading of scripture, had been a great comfort during our first fight. Today's reading from Isaiah was especially comforting, though initially this news seemed to contradict it. This new diagnosis was more than 'nothing at all'; this was inoperable cancer.

Still I was reminded that this illness was not a judgment from God or God breaking a promise; it was another part of the same battle. God was still with us, and surely we still needed God. I came once again to rely on God's grace.

Through the prayers of thousands, the Holy Spirit has turned our fear and doubt into peace and determination. God's promise will hold true—not on our timetable, but God's. All we must do is love and trust.

Prayer: *O God, give us patience, strengthen our faith, and renew our hope when life is difficult. We trust in you for our very lives. Amen*

Thought for the Day: Prayer can change our fear and doubt into peace and determination.

Link2Life: *Pray for and write a note to encourage someone who is ill.*

Ken Franklin (Michigan)

A Blessing in Disguise

Read Acts 20:32–36

Remember the words of the Lord Jesus, how he said, It is more blessed to give than to receive.
Acts 20:35 (KJV)

My last errand for the day was at the supermarket, where I needed to buy only a few items. While I was waiting at the checkout, I began to chat with the older woman in front of me. She was carefully observing the price of each item as it was scanned. Hearing her total, she handed the young cashier a few coins. The cashier counted them and then told her she needed a little more.

The woman, confused, insisted that there was more money in her purse. But searching it, she found none. She then reluctantly removed the eggs from her shopping bag as I slipped the cashier the extra money. Surprised, the woman glanced at me and said, 'What did you do?' I answered her question with a smile and, with tears in her eyes, she said, 'I really needed those eggs. You will be blessed.'

What my new friend didn't realise was that at that moment, I was being blessed. I often think of that woman and wish she could know that although I helped her only momentarily, she permanently blessed me. She gave me the satisfaction of knowing that, even if only for a while, my giving can make a difference for others just as Christ has made a difference for me.

Prayer: *Dear Lord, teach us to listen to your calling. Guide us to extend to others the gifts you have given us. Amen*

Thought for the Day: God, who gives generously to us, wants us to give to others.

Kayci Strickland (Kansas)

PRAYER FOCUS: ELDERLY PEOPLE ON FIXED INCOMES

Christian Friends

Read 1 Samuel 18:1–4; 19:1–7
Jonathan made a covenant with David, because he loved him as his own soul.
1 Samuel 18:3 (NRSV)

Shortly after I became a lay preacher, a member of our church described me as one of his spiritual advisers. Hearing this, I was filled with a great sense of responsibility.

Members of the ancient Celtic church looked for an *anam cara*—a 'soul-friend'. This could be a man or woman, lay or ordained, and experienced in the ways and teachings of Jesus Christ. The soul-friend was someone who could give needed guidance, especially at crucial points in life. Legend has it that Saint Columba's soul-friend suggested that Columba win as many souls for Christ as were lost in a battle he had caused. To do this, Columba left his native Ireland to found a Christian settlement on the Island of Iona, off the west coast of Scotland.

Today, in our own church or Christian community, we can find a soul-friend. Such a friend is someone to whom we can speak openly and honestly, someone who will accompany us on a journey of discovery and help us to follow God more faithfully.

Prayer: *Thank you, Lord, for those who walk beside us, those who help to keep us on your path. We thank you for always walking beside us, leading us forward from morning light until the end of day. Amen*

Thought for the Day: God often guides us through the words of loving friends.

Bill Findlay (Glasgow, Scotland)

Climbing

Read 2 Corinthians 5:6–10

The Lord gives wisdom… guards the course of the just and protects the way of his faithful ones. Then you will understand what is right and just and fair—every good path.
Proverbs 2:6, 8–9 (NIV)

Our family has two teenagers. We enjoy a variety of activities together, especially indoor rock climbing. We have fun challenging ourselves to reach the top. We climb in an old warehouse that has been converted to a climbing facility with more than 30 routes, or climbs, to the ceiling. We take turns climbing and belaying (holding the rope) to keep the climber safe. To climb, we place hands and feet in 'holds' made in the artificial rocks. From the floor, these holds may look too large or too small, easy to reach or too far apart, too smooth or bumpy enough to allow us to grip them. The only way to be sure is actually to ascend the wall, inspect each hold first-hand, and decide which hold is best for your climb.

Our Christian journeys have similar characteristics. We may think we know which tasks are too hard or too easy, which people we can or cannot tolerate, what committees or teams we can or cannot serve on. But until we let God direct our paths and actually begin to act, we cannot understand what 'holds' God may have ready for us to use. Reaching the top of a climbing wall is nothing compared to the joy of working for God's kingdom. God holds the ropes. Let's climb!

Prayer: *Dear God, we pray for courage to act so we can discover where you want us to go, to further your kingdom. Amen*

Thought for the Day: If we're willing to climb, God can take us to new heights.

Lucinda Haag (New York)

Our Spiritual Legacy

Read Deuteronomy 6:4–9

Since my youth, O God, you have taught me, and to this day I declare your marvellous deeds. Even when I am old and grey, do not forsake me, O God, till I declare your power to the next generation, your might to all who are to come.

Psalm 71:17–18 (NIV)

My father died in 1990 at the age of 83. He was a God-fearing man deeply concerned for the spiritual life of his children. We were three brothers and two sisters. He taught us the word of God while we were young. I remember that before going to bed, he would gather us together and tell us the stories of Moses, Joseph, David and Samuel, as well as the parables and miracles of Jesus. This had a tremendous impact on us. From a young age, we knew Jesus and could accept him as our Saviour.

Children are a precious heritage and a wonderful gift from God. Every Christian home can be a theological institute, and parents can be the first ones to speak the word of God to their children. We can introduce them to Jesus when they are young.

Scripture commands us to pass on a spiritual legacy to the next generation. Do we sow God's holy word in the hearts of those we love? This is a great challenge.

Prayer: *Loving God, give us grace to teach your holy word through our words and our actions. Amen*

Thought for the Day: How can I show others my life of prayer?

Jayant S. Trajker (Gujarat, India)

What's in Your Pot?

Read Genesis 1:26—2:3

Six days you shall labour and do all your work, but the seventh day is a Sabbath to the Lord your God. On it you shall not do any work.
Exodus 20:9–10 (NIV)

On a recent Friday afternoon, several new books were donated to the school library where I work. As I entered the books into the library's computer system, I noticed one title I could relate to: *The Empty Pot*. That described exactly how I felt. Hectic schedules, new reports, unanticipated changes and extra classes in the library had left me with nothing left to give. I was tired and empty, like a pot with only bitter dregs at the bottom.

At this time, like so many others, I found refreshment and restoration in my relationship with God through prayer, praise and meditation on God's word.

God demonstrated for us a rhythm of work and rest. Genesis 2:2–3 tells us that after the work of creation was finished, God rested, blessing the seventh day and making it holy. A time of rest is needed and necessary to help us continue our work or service. After difficult workdays and a time of rest, we can face life filled to the brim with God. Then we will be ready and eager to serve those around us with acts of kindness, love and understanding.

Prayer: *Thank you, God, for providing what we need. May we rest and again be filled with your Spirit in Jesus' name. Amen*

Thought for the Day: Resting is not a suggestion; it is a command.

Veneal S. Williams (South Carolina)

The Spirit's Nudge

Read Psalm 23

Yea, though I walk through the valley of the shadow of death, I will fear no evil: for thou art with me.
Psalm 23:4 (KJV)

For some time I have felt a nudge, a desire, to help those in our community who are terminally ill. But recognising the magnitude of the challenge and my own human frailties, I was steadfast in my reluctance to serve. Uncertainty, anxiety and a sense of inadequacy prevented me from stepping out to help those in the final stages of life.

As I prayed about responding to the nudge, I came to realise that God was not asking me to serve alone but promised to be with me. With that assurance, I began to volunteer. I call on God as I travel the busy roads to visit the terminally ill, praying that the Holy Spirit will use me to reveal God's love to my new friends.

Seeing God work in their lives strengthens my spiritual life. I feel God's presence as I rake leaves or mow their lawns or do for them other things they are no longer able to do. I am blessed as they speak to me from their hearts, telling me about regrets, love, blessings, forgiveness and God's walk with them into eternity.

Prayer: *God, help us to realise that we never stand alone, that no matter what the challenges or circumstances of our lives, you are with us. Amen*

Thought for the Day: Where is the Spirit nudging me to serve?

Link2Life: *Find out the needs of a hospice near you and volunteer to meet one of them.*

Doug M. Quinn (Oklahoma)

Sand or Rock?

Read Matthew 7:24–27

Jesus said, 'Everyone… who hears these words of mine and acts on them will be like a wise man who built his house on rock.'
Matthew 7:24 (NRSV)

Today as I read this portion of the Bible, I was reminded of the times that I went to a youth camp on the beach in Somerset, England, many years ago.

One of the activities we looked forward to at this camp was the 'tide fight'. Two teams would build the biggest sandcastle they could on the local beach as the tide was coming in. We would use whatever we could find to make our castle as tall and as strong as possible, to withstand the incoming water. When each castle was complete, a flag was put on the top. Builders of the last castle to fall were the winners. After the tide ebbed, little if anything remained of the castles; they were completely washed away. We had nothing to show for all of the hard work we put into the building of our castles.

Our lives can be like those sandcastles. Jesus said that if we build on sand, the elements will soon destroy what we have built. But if we build on a good and firm base, our buildings will stand up to anything that comes against them. Jesus meant that we are to build our lives on his word, to lay the foundation of our lives on what he taught. That foundation is strong and firm, and it can never be destroyed.

Prayer: *Dear Lord, help us to build on what lasts: your word. We know that we find our strength for living only in you. Amen*

Thought for the Day: On what foundation am I building my life?

John Harrold (Gwent, Wales)

A New Song

Read Psalm 96:1–13

O sing to the Lord a new song; sing to the Lord, all the earth.
Psalm 96:1 (NRSV)

My baby son, John, loves familiar songs. Usually the first time I sing a song to him, he isn't interested. Once he has heard a song several times, hearing it again elicits a big smile.

I too prefer old songs to new ones. In church I feel uncomfortable singing songs I don't know well. Familiar songs are safe. New ones are awkward and risky; I may make a mistake. But new songs give us new ways to praise God. The psalms encourage us to sing 'a new song' to God, to find new ways to 'declare his glory' because 'great is the LORD, and greatly to be praised' (Psalm 96:1, 3, 4).

If we trust God to guide us, we will sometimes leave our comfort zones to do things that we could not do without God. We glorify God by living out the truth that in Christ, we are 'a new creation' (2 Corinthians 5:17). Change may be frightening, but with our mighty God helping us, we can have courage to undertake a new adventure. I sang new songs when I stopped practising law and entered full-time ministry, when I married and when I became a mother. I sing a new song when I set aside old traits such as anger, impatience and self-centeredness for humility, patience and love. Whenever we follow Christ Jesus into an uncertain future, we are singing God's new song.

Prayer: *Source of every song, give us courage to learn new ways to praise you with our life. Amen*

Thought for the Day: What 'new song' is God calling me to sing?

Kristi Iachetta (Texas)

The Grace of Giving

Read 2 Corinthians 8:1–7; 9:6–8

Just as you excel in everything… see that you also excel in this grace of giving.
2 Corinthians 8:7 (NIV)

I re-read the card that contained the generous gift—enough money nearly to pay for a visit to our family in Japan. The widow who gave it to us told us that both the gift and the amount were God's idea and that she was just being obedient. What a blessing to us, and what a lesson for me!

Her faith and generosity challenged my attitude toward giving in general, and money in particular. We are a single-income family, and what I had always considered being 'careful' I now saw as stinginess and lack of faith.

Paul told the Corinthians that God will give us enough to allow us to be generous in every circumstance. This generosity involves not only our attitude toward money but also toward our time, energy, talents and hospitality.

We have the supreme example in Jesus, who gave up everything he had for us so that we might share in everything that he has. We cannot outgive God, who draws on heaven's immense store to give back to us immeasurably more than we have given to others. In doing so, God inspires us to participate in a cycle of generosity.

Prayer: *Dear Father, help us to give cheerfully and to be generous in all things, as you are generous to us. Amen*

Thought for the Day: Generosity is an open-handed, open-hearted approach to all of life.

Link2Life: *Give a gift of time or money to someone who needs it.*

Colette Williams (Tusmore, Australia)

God's Love

Read Psalm 103:1–14

As a father has compassion for his children, so the Lord has compassion for those who fear him. For he knows how we were made; he remembers that we are dust.

Psalm 103:13–14 (NRSV)

I have heard people claim that the God of the Old Testament is a God of wrath and vengeance while the God of the New Testament is a God of love and mercy. But there is only one God in the Bible.

Psalm 103 gives a beautiful description of grace. God's love for me is like my love for my children, only deeper and more perfect. When my children were young, I told them, 'I love you this much' and spread my arms as wide apart as I could. In a similar way, God shows love for us, holding us in one hand and our sins far from us in the other. This loving forgiveness is an undeserved gift.

Our creator knows our limitations. While desiring our best, God is not surprised or thwarted when we fail to live up to the divine hope for us. God's love for us is even more abundant and unconditional than parents' love for their children.

Prayer: *Thank you, God, for your grace and mercy that come to us through Jesus Christ. Amen*

Thought for the Day: God's love extends from everlasting to everlasting.

Mike Macdonald (North Carolina)

You Are Not Locked In!

Read John 8:31–38
'If the Son sets you free, you will be free indeed.'
John 8:36 (NIV)

The company I work for has a large walk-in refrigerator where we keep the fresh fruit we sell. The first time I walked inside the refrigerator to retrieve something, it was so cold I could see my breath in the frigid air and my clothing suddenly felt as flimsy as tissue. I was anxious to get out into warmer air. But when I turned to go out, there was no handle on the door. I began to panic. I was afraid I would freeze to death before someone came to get me out. The manufacturer of the refrigerator must have anticipated this situation; a sign on the inside of the door read, 'You are not locked in!' I then quickly pushed the door open and walked out.

Later, I thought about the times in my life when I've felt locked in spiritually or emotionally with no hope of getting out. At times I was depressed and did not want to go on because I did not think I would ever be happy again. Months of unemployment began to look permanent. Whenever things looked dark and hopeless, God would remind me, 'You are not locked in! I sent my son, Jesus, to set you free.'

By trusting God, praying and reading the Bible, we can find hope that doors will open, healing will come and our hearts and minds will be changed.

Prayer: *Dear God, help us to trust that no matter how trapped we feel, you offer us freedom and fullness of life. Amen*

Thought for the Day: No trap is so strong that God cannot free us from it.

Norma Newton (Oklahoma)

Grow It Alone?

Read Hebrews 10:19–25

Let us consider how to provoke one another to love and good deeds, not neglecting to meet together, as is the habit of some, but encouraging one another, and all the more as you see the Day approaching.
Hebrews 10:24–25 (NRSV)

The weather was windy and humid when I helped a friend plant spring flowers in her flowerbed. 'Plant them close together,' she said. 'These grow better when they're placed that way.' I proceeded to position the small plants with new white blooms in clusters in their new home. Then I began to wonder, 'How will they survive the wind, rain and summer sun? Will they really grow better planted close together?'

As I look over my friend's flower garden months later, the tightly knit group of plants has numerous blooms and is growing. The closeness has worked! Living things need each other to survive and grow.

As Christians, we grow too when we are in community, sharing life with one another. The writer of Hebrews knew the strength of fellowship and that in community believers find encouragement and motivation for love and good deeds. When the winds and storms of life hinder our growth and threaten to beat us down, in community we can face the storms, strengthened by our devotion to Christ and to each other.

Prayer: *O God, help us to encourage and to learn in community with one another. Amen*

Thought for the Day: God does not intend us to grow it alone.

Gina Baldridge (Texas)

My Morning Ritual

Read Matthew 6:5–15

'Whenever you pray, go into your room and shut the door and pray to your Father who is in secret.'
Matthew 6:6 (NRSV)

Many years ago I put into practice something I learned from an article I read in a magazine. The writer had decided to get up an hour earlier in the morning to seek God and had found the experience rewarding.

I decided to do the same. Each morning, I too get up an hour earlier than I used to. I read *The Upper Room* daily devotional for the day, reading the Bible as I meditate in quietness. This early morning hour is also a time of reflection and self-examination that helps to centre me and keep me on God's path. On several occasions, some scripture passages or devotionals seem to have been written specifically for me, to help me through some difficult situation I was facing that very day.

My morning ritual prepares me to get ready for work without rushing, confront the stress of the morning traffic rush in a calm manner, and deal with the decisions I need to make each day. Now I know at least part of the reason Jesus commanded us to 'go into [our] room and shut the door and pray'. How great are the rewards of spending time with God!

Prayer: *God of each morning, from the moment we wake, may we seek your will. Guide our living each day. Amen*

Thought for the Day: At the outset of any journey, seek divine wisdom.

Magdiel Martínez (Nuevo León, México)

Jesus, Our Best Friend

Read John 15:9–17

'I do not call you servants any longer, because the servant does not know what the master is doing; but I have called you friends, because I have made known to you everything that I have heard from my Father.'
John 15:15 (NRSV)

My son, a keen surfer, was thrilled when two world-champion surfers joined him and his friends. The two were attending surfing competitions in Australia, but that morning they had fled the crowds to find a quiet beach. They found the place where my son and his friends had gone for the same reason.

'They treated us as equals, even though they were top surfers,' my son told me in wonder. 'They were real mates.' Surfing with these men was an experience that he will remember for the rest of his life.

His words made me think of Jesus who came to be one of us and treated us as equals. Although he is king of kings, he did not lord it over those he met but came alongside to be a friend and teacher. In fact, what he most desires is deep friendship with each of us.

Prayer: *Dear Lord, give us grace and humility to allow you and our neighbours to serve us. Amen*

Thought for the Day: Jesus is the best friend any of us could ever have.

Dorothy O'Neill (South Australia)

Carry Them to Jesus

Read Mark 2:1–12

Then some people came, bringing to [Jesus] a paralysed man, carried by four of them.

Mark 2:3 (NRSV)

How many sermons have we heard about this paralytic and his four friends? We have made much of their camaraderie. But what if the four weren't the man's friends? What if they didn't know him very well—or even at all? What if one of them just happened to see the paralysed man, recruited three helpers, and carried the man to see Jesus because they believed something good might happen?

My wife and I were told about an 83-year-old woman who lives near us but whom we did not know. She had reared her grandson from infancy and, in his 40s, he had died of cancer. The grandmother was worried sick about being unable to pay the funeral bill.

I spoke to the funeral home, and the staff agreed to reduce the amount owed by 25 per cent if I could raise the rest within two weeks. I called some churches and organisations and told the story to a few friends, and God brought people to help. When I called the grandmother to tell her we had enough money to pay the bill, she could hardly speak. Later my wife and I went to the grandmother's home with the paid-in-full receipt. We stood on the porch, all of us in tears. She could hardly let go of us with her hugs.

God calls us to be present even to the stranger. Were those men the paralytic's friends? I can't prove that they weren't… but you can't prove that they were.

Prayer: *Dear God, open our eyes to your needy world. Amen*

Thought for the day: God calls us to show love and compassion even to strangers.

Gene Cotton (Tennessee)

Spiritual Joy

Read Psalm 19

The Lord has done great things for us, and we are filled with joy.
Psalm 126:3 (NIV)

After a day of rain, a rainbow appeared. I grabbed my camera and hurried on to the seafront balcony. A glorious rainbow spanned several miles of Atlantic coastline. I took several pictures. However, the magnificent rainbow looked like only pale crayon lines in my photographs. I might as well have tried to capture the ocean in a bottle.

Photographs and paintings give us only a hint of the real thing. We fully appreciate the majesty of creation and the emotion it evokes only when we experience it. We come to appreciate God more fully only when we know our Creator firsthand, too. Is that really possible, to know God personally? For many years, I did not think so. I felt disconnected from God. The Bible seemed like ancient history, not God's word.

Fortunately, my family and friends already had personal relationships with God. I listened to their stories of God's blessings in their lives, and I wanted to know God too—to feel God with me every day. I disciplined myself to read my Bible daily. I took several Bible study classes to understand God's laws, lessons and miracles. I explored my many questions about God. Gradually, God became real to me. I confessed my sins, and God blessed me with forgiveness. Then God brought me into a joyful, loving relationship that continues to grow as I continue to study, pray and serve others in Christ's name.

Prayer: *Dear Father, thank you for your love and for bringing us into relationship with you as we seek you through scripture, prayer and serving others. Amen*

Thought for the Day: How am I building a relationship with God?

Deanna Himelick (Florida)

PRAYER FOCUS: THOSE WHO ARE SEARCHING FOR GOD

Off Limits?*

Read Philippians 4:4–9

Let your speech always be gracious, seasoned with salt, so that you may know how you ought to answer everyone.
Colossians 4:6 (NRSV)

Three minutes had elapsed since I had taken my seat at the table. Waitresses and two cooks passed me by, and took no notice of my presence. My ego was soothed only because the truck driver seated next to me was ignored as well.

'Maybe this table is off limits,' I said to him. 'Maybe they are short of staff,' he responded. 'Maybe they don't want our business,' I said. 'Maybe they are looking after those other tables,' was his reply. The hands on the clock continued to move. 'Maybe they don't like us,' I insisted. 'The air conditioning feels so good, I don't mind waiting,' he said.

At this point a harried waitress stopped to tell us that it had been necessary to cut off the water and so the dishwasher was not functioning. My nameless compatriot smiled, thanked the waitress and left. I did not like him. Three times I had sought his support for my obnoxious attitude, but he had let me down. Only later did I realise that he had chosen to practise what I preach.

Prayer: *Dear God, enable us to see ourselves as we really are. Make us sensitive to the trials of others, and let us bring goodwill into life's trying moments. Amen*

Thought for the Day: Whose words do you remember as gracious? What made them so?

Link2Life: *Give special attention today to how you interact with those who serve you.*

Martin E. Pike, Jr. (Texas)

*This is a reprint of a favourite meditation to celebrate the 75th Anniversary of the US edition.

World-Changing Faith

Read James 5:13–18
When [the mob] could not find [Paul and Silas], they dragged Jason and some believers before the city authorities, shouting, 'These people who have been turning the world upside down have come here also.'
Acts 17:6 (NRSV)

We live on the coast. Behind our home is a long strip of rocky beach that ends in a wooded point. The sea curves around the point and forms a quiet inlet between the rocky beach and our land.

One night, a fierce storm blew up. It was too dark to see the ocean, but we could hear the pounding surf. Wind shook the house. Rain pelted the windows. As the tide rose, we prayed that God would calm the storm.

As the sky grew light the next morning, we were astounded to see that the waves had hurled rocks and pebbles from the ocean side of the beach onto the inlet side. Sections of the strip of land were now several feet closer to us than they had been before the storm. The forces of nature change our physical world.

Jesus told his disciples that people of faith can also change the world. Faith, he said, is strong enough to move mountains. Faith is powerful enough to change not only the outward appearance of the world but also us and the way we see the world. Praying can change the way we see our world now, the way we look at things tomorrow, and even the way the past has shaped us. The power of faith is even more far-reaching than the power of nature.

Prayer: *Help us, Lord, to grow stronger in faith as we study your word. Amen*

Thought for the Day: God plants the seed of faith in our hearts.

Kris Wood (Nova Scotia, Canada)

God Our Provider

Read Psalm 104:14–28
The Lord is my shepherd, I shall not want.
Psalm 23:1 (NRSV)

Riots followed the 2007 elections in Kenya. Business stagnated because offices could not open. Food became so expensive that meeting basic needs became difficult. Whether people were self-employed or dependent on daily wages, the story was the same. Putting food on the table for our children was a problem.

It occurred to me that if God can feed the birds of the sky and clothe the lilies of the field, then God could do the same for me and my family. I resorted to prayer and informed the family that God would provide. The following day, a long-time debtor (so distant that we had forgotten about the debt) called to ask how he could pay part of the money he owed me. That day we had a meal on our table, and we gave thanks.

God came to our help in this time of great need.

Prayer: *Dear God, help us to focus on you and not on our problems. Thank you, God, for providing for us. We pray as Jesus taught us, saying, 'Our Father which art in heaven, Hallowed be thy name. Thy kingdom come. Thy will be done, as in heaven, so in earth. Give us day by day our daily bread. And forgive us our sins; for we also forgive every one that is indebted to us. And lead us not into temptation; but deliver us from evil.' (Luke 11:2–4, KJV)*

Thought for the Day: No matter how desperate our situation, God's power is greater.

Link2Life: *To learn how you may help to pray with Africa, go to www.praywithafrica.org.*

Stephen Odhiambo (Nairobi, Kenya)

Big Enough Heart

Read Matthew 5:38–48

God's love has been poured into our hearts through the Holy Spirit that has been given to us.

Romans 5:5 (NRSV)

My church meets in a Christian bookshop near a university campus. Every week, students from all over the world come to the bookshop to hear about God. Many don't know about God and are curious to learn. What they discover often surprises them. One student from China expressed incredulity after hearing that we should love our enemies.

'I think this is a very difficult thing,' she said. 'No one's heart is big enough to do this.'

She had hit upon a profound truth. I responded by telling her she was absolutely right; no one's heart is big enough to love his or her enemies. Only God, whose enormous love is revealed in the creation of human beings, could enable us to carry out such a command. The truth is also a mystery because, although our hearts aren't big enough, God promises to fill our hearts with love through the Holy Spirit. And when we allow our hearts to be filled with God's love, we will find we are able to love our neighbours and even—or perhaps especially—our enemies.

Prayer: *God, thank you for filling our hearts with your love. Now help us to love our enemies. Amen*

Thought for the Day: With God's help we can love our enemies.

Dana Ryan (Arizona)

Unpicked Fruit

Read Galatians 5:16–26

But the fruit of the Spirit is love, joy, peace, patience, kindness, goodness, faithfulness, gentleness and self-control.

Galatians 5:22–23 (NIV)

In our work as Christian leaders, my husband and I have moved house many times during our working lives. Once we moved to a house in Berkshire which had a large garden, part of which was a small orchard with apple, pear and plum trees. Beyond this was a large shed, a greenhouse and more garden.

We arrived in May, and I have to confess that during that first summer I never really looked beyond the shed and the greenhouse. It was not until the following summer that I discovered gooseberry bushes and blackberries. In subsequent years we enjoyed all the fruit in a variety of puddings. But I was ashamed to think of the fruit that had been wasted that first summer. Doubtless the birds enjoyed some of it, but much of it would have rotted on the ground.

God wants us to grow spiritual fruit, such as we read of in Galatians 5. How much are we cultivating daily in our lives? Is our potential to show such fruit in our lives going to waste? I will pray that the fruit of the Spirit will live in me, and be helpful to those I meet each day.

Prayer: *Lord, help us to become better in cultivating the fruit of the Spirit, so that we may be stronger to help others.*

Thought for the Day: That we may make the time to cultivate the fruit of the Spirit in our daily lives.

Barbara Lyne (Dorset, England)

Mistakes in the Bible

Read Romans 5:6–11
Your statutes are wonderful; therefore I obey them.
Psalm 119:129 (NIV)

The open-air preacher stated his theme: 'Mistakes in the Bible'. Someone in the crowd yelled out, 'Good on you, preacher! I always knew there were mistakes in the Bible!'

'Yes,' said the preacher, 'there's the mistake of Adam, the mistake of Cain, the mistake of the rich young ruler. There are so many mistakes, and the people who made them, recorded in the Bible that you'll find your mistake there too!'

The Bible records people's mistakes not only to warn us but to reveal how we can be forgiven for our mistakes and how we can rise above them. The Bible unveils the truth that God doesn't turn a blind eye to our sin. The cross of Christ testifies to the price God paid to forgive us, before and after we became believers.

Living by God's word also has power—power to save us from making mistakes that offend God and hurt ourselves and others. Psalm 119 is dedicated to God in thanksgiving for the Law. The psalmist was thankful. How much more thankful should we be who know the rest of the story, the story of Christ?

Prayer: *Beloved God, may your word light our lives and nourish our spirits. In Jesus' name we pray. Amen*

Thought for the Day: Because of grace, our mistakes can be stepping stones rather than stumbling blocks.

Raymond N. Hawkins (Tasmania, Australia)

PRAYER FOCUS: SOMEONE I HAVE OFFENDED

A Blessings List

Read Lamentations 3:19–26

This I call to mind, and therefore I have hope: The steadfast love of the Lord never ceases, his mercies never come to an end; they are new every morning; great is your faithfulness.
Lamentations 3:21–23 (NRSV)

I sighed as I opened a small notebook where I record prayer requests. Many people I cared about struggled with financial, family or health issues that seemed insoluble. The day's news reported more tragedies around the world. Tears started to fill my eyes. Then I turned to the last page of my prayer notebook. Several years earlier, I began a 'blessings list' of those times I had experienced God's help and presence in a special way. My list included someone's profession of faith, healing, financial provision, and my children finding Christian spouses. As I re-read this list, I remembered that at one time I wasn't sure how or even if God would answer my prayers. But as answers came, I saw God's love and wisdom.

The tears that sometimes come when I pray help me to understand the book of Lamentations. Written about six centuries before Christ's birth, in the last dark days of Judah after it fell to Babylon, the book is full of censure and despair. But tucked within it is a blessings list. When feeling defeated, the writer paused to call to mind God's past faithfulness and declared, in renewed trust: 'Great is your faithfulness.' Lamentations reminds me that answers may not come straight away, but our faithful God sees those who continue to put their hope in our Creator.

Prayer: *Dear Lord, help us to see your light in the darkness of overwhelming circumstances. Amen*

Thought for the Day: God is at work in our most difficult times.

Jeanne Zornes (Washington)

Tasting God's Goodness

Read Psalm 34:1–10

Like newborn babies, crave pure spiritual milk, so that by it you may grow up in your salvation, now that you have tasted that the Lord is good.
1 Peter 2:2–3 (NIV)

The owner of a fruit orchard near me sells fresh peaches. He graciously offers slices of the different varieties for customers to taste. The fruit melts in my mouth. Enjoying the farmer's fruit leads me to spurn shop-bought peaches, which don't compare in sweetness, aroma or flavour with those fresh from the orchard.

Taste gets our attention. Taste raises awareness of more goodness to be enjoyed. The burst of summer fruit in my mouth creates a craving for more. The farmer has confidence in his peaches. He knows that those who taste them will want more.

With similar certainty, Psalm 34:8 urges us to 'taste and see that the Lord is good'. We taste the goodness of God when we live as God asks—and our lives are improved. For example, my wife counselled me to give up bitterness toward my father, who abandoned our family. Resentment toward my dad had become a poison in my soul. When I obeyed God by forgiving my dad, the burden of negativity was lifted from my heart. In trust and obedience, I experienced the help and blessing of God.

Even more than I crave fresh peaches, I hunger for a closer walk with Christ, who offers us abundant life (see John 10:10).

Prayer: *Thank you, God, that as we walk in your ways we taste your goodness. Lead us to share your bounty with others. Amen*

Thought for the Day: How have I tasted God's goodness in my life? Where do I crave more?

Clifford B. Rawley (Missouri)

Banners of Hope

Read Titus 3:3–8
May the God of hope fill you with all joy and peace in believing, so that you may abound in hope by the power of the Holy Spirit.
Romans 15:13 (NRSV)

Churches in our village decided to take part in an initiative called Hope '08. We put up large banners outside each church proclaiming 'There Is Hope'. Sadly, within a few weeks, the banner at the parish church had been stolen. About a month later, a second banner met the same fate. Seemingly, vandals had robbed our village of hope!

This was disappointing and frustrating, but it's wonderful to know that as Christians we will never have our hope stolen. No matter how many setbacks we endure in our lives, no one can rob us of the hope we have in our Saviour, Jesus Christ.

The thieves' efforts to steal our hope have merely reminded us of how great our Saviour is. We still endure doubts, problems and disappointments. But with Christ beside us, we not only have hope for our earthly lives but also a sure and certain hope of eternal life.

Prayer: *Dear God of heaven, thank you that because of Christ we are never without hope. Help us to share that hope with others. Amen*

Thought for the Day: No thief can steal our faith and our hope.

Janet George (Cheshire, England)

Rebirth

Read Ezekiel 37:1–14

I will give you a new heart and a new mind. I will take away your stubborn heart of stone and give you an obedient heart.
Ezekiel 36:26 (GNB)

A film I watched told the story of a man who had died inside and had turned to alcohol to deaden any signs of life. Hope for the future was woefully absent. Then he was hired to be a bodyguard for a charming little girl; and, under her influence, he began to change. He started enjoying life again.

We identify with characters that are reborn. Such characters help us to dream that we can find renewed hope and change.

The good news is that we don't have to settle for vicarious rebirth. The good news is that no matter how many times we have fallen or how far down, we are not beyond God's power to restore us. God knows how to connect bone to bone, to restore flesh and to breathe new life into us. And the best news is that this feeling of life and exhilaration doesn't end as a film does; the vitality that God offers lasts into eternity.

Prayer: *Thank you, God, for your unfathomable power and limitless love. Thank you for your life within us, life that will never end. Amen*

Thought for the Day: No matter what we have done, God can restore us.

Thomas Buice (Florida)

Paying Attention

Read Galatians 6:2–10

In everything do to others as you would have them do to you.
Matthew 7:12 (NRSV)

For days I had been thinking about my mother. I was missing her greatly. She lives in another country, so I am not able to talk to her as frequently as I would like. During this time I received a letter from her telling me how lonely she felt.

I was thinking about my mother one day while preparing supper, when someone knocked at the door. It was Helen, my 83-year-old neighbour who lives alone. I was in a rush to finish preparing my meal, so I hardly paid attention to what she was saying. But all of a sudden I felt God telling me that Helen was like my mother—needing some company, someone to listen to her.

This experience changed my perspective. In the same way that I express love and attention to those around me, God will surely care for my mother. Even though an ocean and many miles separate my mother and me, God will send loving people to attend to her in her time of need—people who are not so busy cooking a meal that they cannot sit down and listen. After all, the Bible teaches us to do for others what we would have them do for us. God's word also calls us to honour our elderly people: 'Rise in the presence of the aged, show respect for the elderly' (Leviticus 19:32, NIV).

Prayer: *Dear Lord, make us aware of the needs of others, and help us to serve them in the name of Christ. Amen*

Thought for the Day: When you're not near the ones you love, love the ones near you.

Link2Life: *Visit an elderly person who has no family nearby.*

Andria D. Amores (Tennessee)

God's Creation

Read Genesis 2:4–15
Blessed be the Lord God of Israel, that made heaven and earth.
2 Chronicles 2:12 (KJV)

According to the account in Genesis, God created the world and called everything good. God made the earth, green and fertile; the birds in the sky; and the fish in the ocean. Animals populate the land. Seasons change, the moon moves through the sky, rain waters the land, crops grow, plants flower and give new seeds. All of creation works together, and the earth contains everything we need.

God created human beings and instructed them to care for the earth and all other living beings. Humans do not play the role of God who created and sustains the earth. But we are responsible for managing our planet, caring for it so that people can live on it.

We are accountable to God for how we treat our land and goods. When corn sprouts and grasses grow, this expresses God's goodness and caring. Every time we use the earth's resources, we have a responsibility to keep the balance God created in the earth's ecosystems.

Many believers around the world have begun to recognise that we are accountable for the way we live—as God told us in the beginning.

Prayer: *Dear God, teach us to be good stewards of your creation. Amen*

Thought for the Day: We have the Earth on loan. How can we care for it?

Thomas Risager (Syddanmark, Denmark)

One Day at a Time

Read Matthew 6:25–34

'Do not worry about tomorrow, for tomorrow will worry about itself. Each day has enough trouble of its own.'
Matthew 6:34 (NIV)

I have been battling cancer for over a year now, hoping the spots on my liver would be gone or at least reduced in size. My latest CAT scan revealed that the spots had neither shrunk nor grown. I am thankful that my condition is stable.

I am learning to live one day at a time, which has never been easy for me. My brother once dubbed me 'Mr Five-Year Plan'. Now I find it hard to look ahead five days.

Yet I am blessed. People pray for me, provide financial assistance and encourage me. While I need to budget my energy, I still work at a day job and also keep active with my work as an actor and writer. Some people say they're amazed at all I do.

But I know I keep going only by the grace of God. I knew from the beginning I couldn't do it alone, that I would need to rely on God to be my healer and provider. El Shaddai, one of the Hebrew names for God, means 'the all-sufficient God', the God of more than enough. By trusting that God is enough, I can take life one day at a time.

Prayer: *Help us, O Lord, to live for this day, this hour, this moment. Amen*

Thought for the Day: Let tomorrow worry about itself; today, live.

Gordon Williams (Texas)

The Right Gift

Read 1 Corinthians 12:4–7
Do not neglect the gift that is in you.
1 Timothy 4:14 (NRSV)

My father loves roses. Once after he moved into a new house, he planted twelve rose bushes. To celebrate, my sister and I each sent him a gift. I sent a green plastic bucket to hold kitchen scraps until he could put them on his compost heap. She sent a crystal bud vase.

Our gifts reveal something about each of us. My sister is elegant; I am practical. But Dad assured us, 'Both of your gifts are equally needed and equally welcome.'

Our heavenly parent is like my dad. God does not expect the same from all of us. Because God made us and made us different, God delights in us just as we are. God wants each of us to offer the gifts that best express who we are and what we have to give.

Prayer: *Dear God, lead us to discover the gifts you have planted within us so that we can give our best to you and to your kingdom. As Jesus taught us, we pray, 'Our Father which art in heaven, Hallowed be thy name. Thy kingdom come. Thy will be done in earth, as it is in heaven. Give us this day our daily bread. And forgive us our debts, as we forgive our debtors. And lead us not into temptation, but deliver us from evil: For thine is the kingdom, and the power, and the glory, for ever. Amen.' (Matthew 6:9–13, KJV)*

Thought for the Day: God made us and loves us as we are.

Patricia H. Sprinkle (Georgia)

A Divine Whisper

Read 1 Kings 19:1–13
Be still, and know that I am God.
Psalm 46:10 (NIV)

Flowers and candles decorated the hall. Wonderful smells of food cooking drifted in from the kitchen. Laughter and happy faces promised enjoyable fellowship for the women of our church. My friend and I could sit together and chat. Unfortunately, I could hardly hear a word she said because in the corner, speakers blared out 'background' music. I leaned forward and studied my friend's lips. Her hands waved as she described an event, but to my frustration I couldn't follow her story. If only I could have turned the speaker volume down or even put my ear closer to my friend's mouth! As it was, I heard only a few words and so received a confusing, partial message because of the background noise.

Many times I pray and listen for God's response but don't receive the guidance I long for. I wonder how often that's because I can't hear God's voice over the background noise in my life. I rush from task to task, stopping occasionally to utter a quick prayer—then wonder why God doesn't seem to hear and answer.

But I'm fairly certain the problem isn't on God's side. When we step out of our busyness and draw near to God we will be better able to hear God's guidance—even when it comes in a whisper.

Prayer: *Loving God, thank you that you want to speak to us. Help us to listen for your voice, even when it's only a whisper. Amen*

Thought for the Day: What prevents me from hearing God?

Link2Life: *Spend two minutes in silence today, not praying but listening.*

Shirley M. Corder (Eastern Cape, South Africa)

Walk in Love

Read 1 Corinthians 13

Be imitators of God, as beloved children, and live in love, as Christ loved us and gave himself up for us.
Ephesians 5:1–2 (NRSV)

I have been in prison since 1990, and over the years I have found myself in some difficult situations. Whenever trouble arises, applying biblical principles can bring about a peaceful resolution. One principle I have lived by throughout the duration of my imprisonment is always to walk in love.

A few years ago, I had an opportunity to practise this principle when another prisoner started to hassle me about my faith. Whenever he saw me he would make derogatory remarks about Christians. This went on for a few months. With each encounter, I walked in love, rejoiced in my persecutions (Matthew 5:11–12) and prayed for my persecutor (Matthew 5:44).

One day, during another encounter with this person, I politely interrupted him while he was still speaking. I felt there was something he needed to know. 'My friend,' I said, 'nothing you ever say to me or do to me will stop me from loving you.' He stood speechless as I walked away. A few days later he saw me standing in the hallway. 'Jeff, I haven't slept since you told me you loved me the other day. That's exactly what Jesus would have told me. You're a real Christian. Please forgive me for the way I've treated you,' he said remorsefully. Now, I was speechless! Since then, he has never spoken another unkind word to me.

Prayer: *Dear Father, help us to walk always in love. Amen*

Thought for the Day: No matter how difficult our situation, with God's help we can see ways to show God's love.

Jeff Matthews (Indiana)

God Is the Director

Read Proverbs 16:1–3
Cast all your anxiety on him, because he cares for you.
1 Peter 5:7 (NRSV)

On my patio, where I say my morning prayers and study my Bible, is a white director's chair. On the canvas, written in big red letters, are the words 'God Is the Director'. I had the chair made because I wanted to see the message as a daily reminder.

I tend to forget that God is the one in charge. As a wife and mother, I sometimes want to direct my husband and my children. As an employee, I often think I know better than my boss. I disagree with people, neighbours and politicians. But trying to be the director destroys my peace. While I sometimes have the right or the duty to express my ideas, I can't make anyone act on them.

My chair reminds me to give all my cares and concerns to God. God is not only my director, but the director of all our lives. God is running the show, not me.

Daily, I ask God for my script. I don't worry about the parts other people are playing. I let God direct them. I tell God my concerns, and I ask what he wants me to do. Most of the time, God tells me to let go.

When I'm the director, the show doesn't always turn out well. Letting God be the director ensures the best show for everyone.

Prayer: *Dear God, help us remember that you know what is best. Amen*

Thought for the Day: God is the director; I will ask him for direction.

Gail Griner Golden (Florida)

Summer and Winter

Read Ecclesiastes 3:1–13

The Lord says, 'Even to your old age I am he, even when you turn grey I will carry you.'
Isaiah 46:4 (NRSV)

In South Africa in July, winter is fully upon us. This season brings dry, khaki-coloured grass, bone-hard ground and frosty cold mornings interspersed with relatively warm days. We have, attentively or not, made the transition through autumn to winter. The unstable weather that came with the change is left behind as the season matures.

It is much the same with us. We are perpetually either in a season or between seasons in our personal lives, our church and community, our nations; and the time between these seasons often unsettles us. Our nation experienced this when we elected our new president. But also as often happens, this unsettled time has led to great creativity, with many new ideas being put forward to address pressing national concerns.

Whatever season we are in, our loving God continues to send us goodness to enjoy. Every stage of life brings fruits to remind us of God's presence and to make us thankful. Most of all, these gifts remind us that God loves each of us with an unmatched, unrivalled intensity, every day.

Prayer: *Generous God, open our eyes to the treasures today brings.*

Thought for the Day: In every season of life, God gives gifts to be savoured.

Link2Life: *Read about a country you are unfamiliar with and pray for its people.*

Roland Rink (Gauteng, South Africa)

A Divine Spark

Read Romans 12:4–8
Now there are diversities of gifts, but the same Spirit.
1 Corinthians 12:4 (KJV)

We may readily recognise inspiration in the work of artists, musicians and writers, but we usually stop short of seeing simple acts of kindness as inspired. I had the privilege of seeing my sister-in-law act as a link between my father's need and God's mercy. My father was admitted to a nursing home for care after suffering a stroke. Limited to using his right side, my father requires assistance with his basic needs.

One night she breezed into the room cheerfully. She immediately set about anticipating and responding to my father's needs. It is not always easy to get past his veneer of gruffness, but she has found a way. In the time it took me to juggle toothbrush and water cup, she had wrestled a partially paralysed man out of his soiled shirt and into a fresh one, finishing by folding his blanket back in just the way he likes it.

I had heard what a great blessing my sister-in-law had been in caring for my father, but witnessing it firsthand opened my eyes to her deeply compassionate heart. We are all given a spark of the Holy Spirit that ignites when we engage in a work where our passion lies.

Prayer: *Thank you, God, for sending helpers to us at our points of need. Bless them as they dispense your mercy and show your compassion. Amen*

Thought for the Day: Our 'ordinary' acts can serve God and others.

Carol P. Nyborg (North Carolina)

Rocks of God

Read 2 Timothy 1:3–5

It was your faith that encouraged us, because now we really live if you stand firm in your life in union with the Lord.

1 Thessalonians 3:7 (GNB)

Following the paths that the poet William Wordsworth walked around Grasmere, his loved home in the Lake District, it was not difficult to share his love of nature. I watched and listened to his sounds, 'of waters rolling from their mountain springs'. The previous night's rain had produced a torrent of water rushing over rocks and stones, creating its own nature-music. A deep bass throbbing undercurrent was topped by a trilling ripple and a persistent drip-drip into a rocky pool. A thrilling orchestra of sound held me enraptured by the same eternal beauty that the poet had captured in his lines.

The stones themselves, both rocky banks and pebbles in the stream, are mostly silent, but without them, far downstream, the still waters lose their melody. I thought of the 'silent stones' in my life—the people who have enabled me to minister in Christ's name: parents, family, teachers, friends. They have not all made vibrant music to be acclaimed by others, but by their presence, their godly example and advice, have helped me to live and preach and write with a richer sound. These rocks of God are often silent, but it is they who make life's music.

Prayer: *Lord, when life seems full of happy music and all is well, let me remember and give thanks for those who have helped me write the score.*

Thought for the Day: I am surrounded by rocks of God.

Colin D. Harbach (Carlisle, England)

Love from the One for All

Read James 2:1–5

If we love one another, God lives in us and his love is made complete in us.
1 John 4:12 (NIV)

On the Sunday before Easter, the stranger appeared at church reeking of alcohol after drinking heavily. The congregation invited him to stay for the Palm Sunday service, which began with the people joyfully waving palms. Walking with uncertain step, the visitor caught on and waved his palm heartily.

Before the sermon, the congregation greeted one another with a sign of peace. The visitor seemed genuinely blessed as each person took his hands, looked into his eyes, and said, 'The peace of God be with you.' But then he restlessly ambled around the church. No one knew what to do.

After several minutes, a woman went to the visitor, took his hand and asked, 'Would you like to come and sit with me?' He responded to her gentleness and sat attentively through the service. Only weeks before, that kind woman had told the pastor of her inordinate fear of strangers. They prayed that God would help her to overcome her fear. Fears are real, but the kind of love God gives can nudge out, expel and conquer fear.

Prayer: *O God, help us to welcome strangers with your love. Amen*

Thought for the Day: When has your congregation welcomed a stranger?

Ron Barham* (Mississippi)

PRAYER FOCUS: FAMILIES OF THOSE WHO DRINK TOO MUCH
*Mr Barham died while this issue was in production.

A Thankful Heart

Read Luke 17:11–19
He prostrated himself at Jesus' feet and thanked him.
Luke 17:16 (NRSV)

One of my friends was diagnosed with cancer. He was frightened and didn't know what to do. On advice, he went to church and prayed; and after some time, he felt some relief. The next time he had a doctor's appointment, the doctor told him that he was healthy. But he did not go to the church and thank God. He said, 'I don't think I was ever ill. They got my test results mixed up with someone else's. I have nothing to thank God for.'

In the story of the ten lepers, I was struck by the words, 'He prostrated himself at Jesus' feet and thanked him.' When my friend thought he was ill, he agreed that he needed God. But once he found that he was not ill, he forgot about God.

Jesus healed all ten lepers, but only one turned back to thank him. The leper who came back in gratitude had received both physical and spiritual healing. He praised God.

Prayer: *Thank you, God. You are the reason for our existence and for all the blessings of our lives. Help us to recognise our need for you and to offer you our thanks for all the good that comes to us, as we pray, 'Our Father in heaven, hallowed be your name, your kingdom come, your will be done on earth as it is in heaven. Give us today our daily bread. Forgive us our debts, as we also have forgiven our debtors. And lead us not into temptation, but deliver us from the evil one.' (Matthew 6:9–13, NIV)*

Thought for the Day: Gratitude is the sign of a changed heart.

Nadezhda Popova (Komi Republic, Russia)

A Walk in the Sun

Read 1 John 1:5–7

Jesus said, 'I am the light of the world. Whoever follows me will never walk in darkness, but will have the light of life.'
John 8:12 (NIV)

My days begin with a walk along our country road. Because of the changing seasons, sometimes the sun is already high in the sky as I walk. At other times, it is still dark. But at certain times of the year, I walk toward the rising sun. As the tremendously bright ball comes up over the horizon, it seems overwhelming in its brightness. I am tempted to just turn and return home, walking away from that dazzling light. However, I have discovered that as I continue my walk, the sun moves higher and lights the road, showing me the rough and smooth places.

When I seek God through prayer a similar thing happens. God's power seems overwhelming. It is hard to believe that God could care about my small, human joys and problems. Yet when I share my thoughts with God in prayer, I find it easier to see how to go about my daily tasks. I can deal more confidently with my challenges, just as I can walk more confidently when the sun lights the road.

Prayer: *Dear God, thank you for caring about our problems. Continue to show us the way. Amen*

Thought for the Day: If we ask, God will always light our way.

Pat Gamage (Michigan)

God is in Control

Read Isaiah 58:6–12

Treat them as you would an Israelite, and love them as you love yourselves. Remember that you were once foreigners in the land of Egypt. I am the Lord your God.
Leviticus 19:34 (GNB)

At a time of horrendous xenophobia in my country, South Africa, we see and hear of atrocities perpetrated by our fellow South Africans against people from other African countries. At such a time we might well ask, 'Where is God?'

At times like these our faith can show its true colours. For every 'why' we can answer in our own hearts, 'We don't understand Lord, but we still believe.' Every 'why' brings an opportunity for our faith to grow.

Perhaps this outlook is easier for us than for 'the foreigners' who are on the receiving end of the violence. But in situations like these we all have something to do. We can pray, and we can help the one, two or more that we can. We can give shelter, food and comfort, as Isaiah told God's people: 'Remove the chains of oppression… let the oppressed go free. Share your food with the hungry and open your homes to the homeless poor' (Isaiah 58:6–7).

We should not be afraid to let our light shine for fear of how doing so might affect our lives. Let us have the faith to trust God in all circumstances and the courage to do our part as we become co-workers with God.

Prayer: *O God, when we don't understand, help us to trust you anyway. And give us courage to right the wrongs we see close at hand. Amen*

Thought for the Day: Don't fret about the wrongs you see; act to bring God's justice.

Elaine Richardson (Western Cape, South Africa)

Harvest

Read Psalm 126

Those who go out weeping, bearing the seed for sowing, shall come home with shouts of joy, carrying their sheaves.
Psalm 126:6 (NRSV)

In the spring of 2001, I began leading a women's Bible study in the church where my husband was the pastor. Our group started with around a dozen women; more joined in the autumn session. Six weeks into the second study, my husband died suddenly. One week after his funeral, I went back to leading the study. My motive was not particularly noble. I needed to return to some sort of normality; and I knew these wonderful women, whom I had grown to love, would be a support for me.

During that study, we bonded in a way that does not often happen in good times. As I honestly talked about my grief, my doubts and my anger with God, the women talked about their deepest feelings. One person commented that I was the strongest woman she had ever known; I remember thinking, 'I don't feel very strong.' During many of the sessions, though I was the leader, their strength carried me.

Our group eventually grew to more than 40 women, and God alone deserves the credit. I believe God used my honesty when I was floundering to produce fruit I never could have anticipated. Even the weakest among us can spread the good news that God is always faithful.

Prayer: *Dear God, when our struggles make us want to pull away from other people, help us to be honest and to keep on serving. Amen*

Thought for the Day: Talking honestly about our doubts can lead to deeper faith.

Sandy Sheppard (Michigan)

The Sparrow

Read Matthew 10:29–31

Jesus said, 'Not one [sparrow] will fall to the ground apart from the will of your Father.'
Matthew 10:29 (NIV)

As a keen birdwatcher, I often long for some spectacular species to come to my bird feeder, while often dismissing the common birds with scarcely a glance. That was true until I happened on a little sparrow, that most familiar of birds, which had been stunned by a passing vehicle and was lying on the road. I quickly rescued the bird and gently carried it home. Looking at it closely, I was amazed by its beauty. Its back was a beautiful, rich chestnut colour with black stripes, and its wings were brown with a lovely white bar. Its head was grey, and its chest and abdomen were fluffy and white. I marvelled at the delicate feet that can hold this frail-looking little bird to a twig in the fiercest of gales. As I cupped its tiny body in my hand, the faint heartbeat against my palm made me cry.

The Bible says that God knows when a sparrow falls to the ground. God had watched this particular sparrow fall to the ground, had watched me pick it up and was with us now in this moment. I realised that, like the sparrow lovingly sheltered in my hand, I am held in the palm of God's hand. God speaks tender words to me and tells me I am loved, approved and valued beyond measure.

Prayer: *Dear heavenly Father, thank you for your amazing, unconditional love for all your creatures—especially me. Amen*

Thought for the Day: Our names are written on God's hands (see Isaiah 49:16).

Janice Ross (Orkney Islands, Scotland)

PRAYER FOCUS: THOSE WHO NEED TO KNOW GOD LOVES THEM

Called to Care

Read Psalm 71:17–21

Remember your leaders, those who spoke the word of God to you; consider the outcome of their way of life, and imitate their faith.
Hebrews 13:7 (NRSV)

Bill was my dad's partner in a car-parts business. After World War II, with nothing but sheer determination, the two of them started the company. They sold to petrol stations, car dealerships and people who worked on their own cars all over our area.

People also knew that they were faithful church members. Dad taught a Sunday school class of senior-high boys. Teaching wasn't exactly his strongest spiritual gift, but he gave it a good try, and the boys seemed to appreciate it. Bill was the adult counsellor for the youth fellowship, which fit his sense of humour. Their careers were in car parts, but their calling was in making disciples of Jesus Christ.

While there are still people in that small town who remember Bill and my dad because of what they did with their business, there are also former teenagers, now grandparents, who give thanks for the way the two men helped lead them to Christ.

That's why reaching out to young people matters. It's hard to imagine anything more challenging than being a Christian teenager in today's culture. But amid the cacophony of conflicting voices that would lead young people in a multitude of different directions, we can celebrate what God is doing in and through the lives of those who work with young people.

Prayer: *We give you thanks, O God, for those who bring your word of love and truth to young people. Amen*

Thought for the Day: Young people face difficult choices every day. Pray for them.

Jim Harnish (Florida)

Passion and Compassion

Read Colossians 3:1-12

As God's chosen ones, holy and beloved, clothe yourselves with compassion, kindness, humility, meekness and patience.
Colossians 3:12 (NRSV)

It was a very hot Thursday, about 8.00 p.m. Traffic was intense. Cars and buses were not moving. Thunder announced a coming storm. Everything was dark except the lights of the vehicles, since we had been without power in our neighbourhood for some time. In the midst of this, an ambulance siren wailed. From my vantage point at the door of the church, I could see someone in the ambulance—perhaps a doctor or nurse—trying to help someone. The ambulance driver frantically waved his hand outside the window, pleading for people to let him get through.

I thought, 'If that were me in that ambulance, I would like to be cared for with the intensity I saw in that crew, by people who would fight for my life.' Instantly, I thought of the church as something like the intensive care unit of a hospital. We are called, made capable and sustained by God to fight for God's people—so that they may have abundant life, life guided by God's saving love and grace. God wants a church that acts with passion and compassion so that those the world injures may find their true worth as children of God.

Prayer: *Loving God, we want to be a church that grows closer to Christ in everything, consecrated by him to love and serve those the world has forgotten, for your glory. Amen*

Thought for the Day: People of faith are God's caring presence in the world.

Ronan Boechat de Amorim (Rio de Janeiro, Brazil)

The God Who Searches

Read Ezekiel 33:10–16

The Son of Man came to seek out and to save the lost.
Luke 19:10 (NRSV)

For three years, while I studied at theological college, I preached every Saturday at the central prison in San José. One Saturday, I travelled to the prison as usual. This time, however, due to an intensely busy work week, I did not have a message prepared. I pleaded with God to help me. As I was walking along, I saw Blue on the street corner, searching through the rubbish bins. Blue is an elderly man known to everyone in the area. He searches through the bins, looking for blue objects to recycle—hence his nickname. At that moment, I knew what the Bible reference and the theme of my message would be; I would talk about the God who unfailingly seeks us.

The message was not lost on the prisoners. They understood that, like Blue who recycles items of value from the rubbish bins, Christ searches for us, rescues us and offers us salvation because we are valuable in God's sight.

Several prisoners accepted Christ that day, which changed the lives of many of them. One, who had been condemned to a life sentence, later gained his freedom and returned to his hometown, where he formed a new church.

Prayer: *Thank you, God, for rescuing us, for loving us unconditionally, and for giving us eternal life through Jesus Christ. Amen*

Thought for the Day: God continually searches for those who need to meet Christ.

Gilberto Valencia (Cali, Colombia)

Life in Order

Read Romans 8:35–39

If we live, it is for the Lord that we live, and if we die, it is for the Lord that we die. So whether we live or die, we belong to the Lord.
Romans 14:8 (GNB)

'Everything is fine,' said my sister-in-law to me as she lay dying. My mind swirled with questions. She was only 65 years old, recently retired, with a loving and supportive family. After five years of battling breast cancer, she was dying. How could everything be fine?

During her funeral, when the minister read from Romans 8:35–39, I realised the meaning of her last words to me: she was saying that nothing can separate us from the love of God, not even death. My sister-in-law looked beyond earthly concerns and placed her faith and trust in God's love. Even though we can become overwhelmed by worldly concerns, nothing is as powerful as the love of God in our hearts.

As Christians, we seek God's guidance to put our lives in order; we can live each day as if it were our last. Scripture assures us that 'nothing in all creation… will ever be able to separate us from the love of God which is ours through Christ Jesus our Lord' (Romans 8:39).

Prayer: *Loving God, may we feel your presence in all that we do each day. Help us to keep our lives in order to better serve you. Amen*

Thought for the Day: Not even death can separate us from God.

Lynda S. Phillips (Tennessee)

Stepping Out in Faith

Read Matthew 14:22–33

Peter spoke up. 'Lord, if it is really you, order me to come out on the water to you.' 'Come!' answered Jesus. So Peter got out of the boat and started walking on the water to Jesus.
Matthew 14:28–29 (GNB)

On a recent mission trip to Honduras, I was aware that several members of the team were on their first such trip. They were anxious about their assigned task, reaching out to people who were poor and who spoke a language we didn't understand. In our devotional time the first night, I read Matthew 14:22–33. I hoped to convey that, like Peter, at times we must get out of our boat, leaving what is comfortable for us in order to do God's work. Taking that first step is scary, but it leads to many blessings. Once he stepped out in faith, Peter had an opportunity to walk on water, to be lifted up, to be taught, to be touched by the Master. Peter recognised Jesus coming toward them and saw an opportunity to join him.

Like Peter when we step out in faith, we open a door for God to work. We may perform tasks, experience the results of a concerted team effort we would not dream of doing on our own, or receive a hug or a smile from someone whose language we don't understand. We are offered opportunities to step out of our boats and walk toward Jesus. Once we take that step, we will never be the same.

Prayer: *Gracious and loving God, help us to step out in faith when we hear your call to reach out to others. Amen*

Thought for the Day: If we want to walk on water, we have to get out of the boat.

Link2Life: *Volunteer to do something new in your church or community.*

J. Ken Stringer (Mississippi)

Comfort My Heart

Read Isaiah 40:9–11

After you have suffered for a little while, the God of all grace, who has called you to his eternal glory in Christ, will himself restore, support, strengthen and establish you.

1 Peter 5:10 (NRSV)

Being on crutches and unable to drive was frustrating for me. Friends were helpful, however, and made sure I got where I needed to go: church, Bible study, the doctor and the supermarket.

Returning after one outing, as I made slow progress up the stairs to my flat, my friend followed closely. With each step, she lightly placed her hand on my back.

'Your hand is comforting,' I said. 'It steadies me.'

Often we find ourselves in circumstances where we need comfort. God, like a shepherd tending a flock with a staff, places a hand on us. God touches our hearts when we need it most, and we feel more at peace. God's peace keeps us steady in our trials. We're able to move through difficult times, overcoming temptation, doubt and fear.

Sometimes God's comfort comes in the form of the written word. We may receive help and support from another believer. Many times God speaks through the Spirit in answer to prayer. However the help comes, we can always trust that God's comfort will steady us.

Prayer: *Dear Lord, help us to remember that you offer the peace and comfort we need to get through life's trials. Amen*

Thought for the Day: God's steadying hand is always near.

Link2Life: *Help someone who is recovering from surgery or injury.*

Paula Geister (Michigan)

The World is Waiting for You

Read Philippians 1:3–11

I am confident of this, that the one who began a good work among you will bring it to completion by the day of Jesus Christ.
Philippians 1:6 (NRSV)

Catherine Booth was the wife of General William Booth, founder of the Salvation Army. Reportedly, in the course of rearing her large family, Catherine would often tell her children: 'Now remember, you are not here in this world for yourselves. You have been sent—for God and for others. The world is waiting for you.' Consequently, they grew up with a very clear picture of their Christian calling and took an active part in Christian ministry.

God has a specific purpose for each of us as we follow in the footsteps of Jesus, who declared that he came not to be served but to serve. Christ Jesus is our perfect example—giving himself in obedience to God for the sake of others, both in his life and in his death. The apostle Paul's prayer was that the Christians of ancient Philippi would continue increasing in love, knowledge and insight as they passed on the Good News of Christ. Paul was confident that their obedience to the Lord's call would bring a rich harvest.

God has entrusted us with the role of passing on the gospel to a waiting world in our day. What a privilege and responsibility!

Prayer: *Dear Lord, empower us to show the waiting world your mercy and forgiveness. Amen*

Thought for the Day: How are you answering God's call in your life?

Hazel V. Thompson (Somerset, England)

Restored

Read Acts 3:11–16

You also, like living stones, are being built into a spiritual house to be a holy priesthood, offering spiritual sacrifices acceptable to God through Jesus Christ.

1 Peter 2:5 (NIV)

On my street sits an empty, Georgian-style house with huge white columns in front. As I pass by this old house, I think how beautiful it must have been in times past. It has been neglected for many years; the paint is fading and peeling. The house has been vandalised inside and out. It's hard to know how much damage has been done. 'How much would it cost to restore this old house?' I wondered. 'Can it even be saved?' How I wish someone would move in and renovate the old place! I know it has the potential to be beautiful again.

That old house is a lot like many of us. We come into this world created by our Maker to be whole. Then someone we trust hurts us emotionally, physically or both. We may shut off our emotions because it hurts too much to feel. Spirits are broken and sometimes even destroyed. Others may start to wonder if we can ever be restored. But when we allow Christ Jesus into our hearts, he can heal the scars caused by life and repair our wounded spirit. And unlike that old house on my street that could be too costly to restore, the high price of our restoration has been paid by Christ, the Master Carpenter, whose work is always of highest quality.

Prayer: *Father, thank you for your assurance that faith in Jesus Christ can bring us complete healing. Amen*

Thought for the Day: We are never so broken that God cannot restore us.

Susan Dollyhigh (North Carolina)

Interruptions

Read 1 Samuel 3:1–10

Speak, Lord, for your servant is listening.
1 Samuel 3:9 (NRSV)

As a high-school teacher, I am frequently interrupted by announcements over the school's intercom system. Often the interruption involves a student being called to the office or a change in an athletic team's practice schedule. To me, these announcements constituted an annoying interruption of valuable teaching time. However, when I read about the priest Eli and the boy Samuel in the Bible, I suddenly saw these daily interruptions in a new way.

Eli's sleep was interrupted three times by Samuel because Samuel thought that Eli was calling him. Eli thought Samuel's interruptions were simply a child disturbing his sleep, until he realised that Samuel was being called by God.

Reading about Eli's misinterpretation of Samuel's interruptions, I wondered if I was misinterpreting those intercom interruptions. Perhaps the interruptions were God's call to me to pray for the student or athletic team in question. Once I began to treat the intercom interruptions as calls to prayer, they were no longer an annoyance. I won't say that I look forward to the interruptions, but instead of being annoyed by them I now channel that energy into prayer.

Prayer: *Dear God, help us to remember to look for you in both the routine tasks and the interruptions of our daily life. In Jesus' name we pray. Amen*

Thought for the Day: How can I make life's annoyances into calls to prayer?

Link2Life: *Each time you are interrupted today, stop and pray.*

Vicki Hines (Tennessee)

Witnesses

Read 2 Corinthians 1:3–7
Praise be to the God and Father of our Lord Jesus Christ, the Father of compassion and the God of all comfort.
2 Corinthians 1:3 (NIV)

Terminally ill patients often know when death is near, yet I couldn't tell if Delores was just being overly positive. 'I'm not ready to die,' she said. 'I'm going home.' A nurse had paged me, the on-call chaplain, because she thought Delores was about to die.

But Delores did go home, only to return for more chemo, more radiation. When I stopped to see her one morning, I barely recognised her from the effects of her treatment. Suddenly, she exclaimed, 'He was here, right here in my room.'

'Who was?' I asked.

'Jesus! I was lying here in bed, and I looked up at that wall over there and—' She stopped. Her eyes filled with tears as she pointed toward the wall opposite her bed. 'Jesus came through that wall. The room was flooded with light, and it was so peaceful! Thank you, Jesus!'

I found her joy so palpable that I started to cry. You can't work in a hospital among the critically ill and dying without struggling with God. In Delores' presence, I felt with my whole being that what we Christians say and hope and pray is true. The one who once walked among us, the one who died on the cross, is risen. He is faithful and will not leave us comfortless. Sometimes it takes someone else's faith to remind us of that.

Prayer: *O God, thank you for coming to us in our need and empowering us to live faithfully. Amen*

Thought for the Day: What we say and hope is true: Christ is risen.

Marcia Krause Bilyk (New Jersey)

What We Least Expect

Read Acts 3:1–10

Peter said [to the man], 'I have no silver or gold, but what I have I give you; in the name of Jesus Christ of Nazareth, stand up and walk.'
Acts 3:6 (NRSV)

When my children were young and wanted a new toy, I often heard, 'But Mum, I need it!' As children of our heavenly Father, we are no different. Sometimes what we perceive as our greatest need is not at all what we need.

In today's reading from Acts 3 the beggar who was laid at the temple gate thought his greatest need was money. He had been crippled since birth and had no way to earn income for life's necessities. Consequently, he had begged for money.

Had Peter and John given the man money, his immediate need would have been met, but his life would not have changed. The next day he would have been back at the gate again, begging. Instead, Peter looked at the man's greater need—his need for physical and spiritual healing. The beggar left the gate that day a changed man, praising God. He could walk! He received not what he asked for but what he needed.

Our wise God often goes beyond what we ask, too. Many years ago, I prayed for God to move my husband to a particular job. It didn't happen. In the time since, that organisation has endured years of staff changes and upheaval. God, in mercy, sent us to a different place, to a job that has been stable for 13 years.

Prayer: *Dear Father, thank you for meeting our deep needs, even when what comes to us is not what we expected. Amen*

Thought for the Day: God can work through us to meet the deepest needs of those near us.

Cathy Bryant (Texas

Telling the Truth

Read Ephesians 4:25—5:2

Jesus said, 'They who have my commandments and keep them are those who love me; and those who love me will be loved by my Father, and I will love them and reveal myself to them.'

John 14:21 (NRSV)

For a long time I thought that small lies were something common and sometimes good. I used to think that they helped me in my life. However when I began reading God's word and other Christian books regularly, I realised that I was wrong.

The Lord wants us to obey the Bible's commands to be truthful and its other guidance as well. Our obedience witnesses to our faith and expresses that we do love God. When we obey God, we can overcome difficulties in our life. I decided that with God's help I could change and resolve to always be truthful. And the Holy Spirit helped me. Now I read the Bible regularly, pray every day, try to listen more carefully to God's voice and speak less. I ask Christ to help me learn more every day what he wants to teach me.

Prayer: *Thank you, God, that you love us, even though we are sinners. Help us to be close to you and to follow you. Amen*

Thought for the Day: We embody the truth of Christ when we live by his commands.

Nikola Shopov (Varna, Bulgaria)

The Legacy

Read Romans 4:13–25

By faith [Abraham...] was enabled to become a father because he considered him faithful who had made the promise.

Hebrews 11:11 (NIV)

When my father died in 2003, what had been his for 87 years became mine because I was his heir. I inherited it.

In his letters, the apostle Paul used the language of inheritance to connect Abraham and the Christians in Rome. Believers had become heirs of Abraham's best gift, his faith. All of us come into God's family—become God's heirs —not because of genetics but by belief. Just as Abraham was counted righteous because of his faith, we become God's children by faith in Jesus Christ (see John 1:12–13).

Abraham is long gone, but the opportunity to believe remains. Faith is the determining factor for anyone, anytime, anywhere. Faith is multi-racial, multi-cultural and multi-denominational. We differ in many ways, but we all are welcome in the family 'by faith'.

The greatest thing my dad left me was the legacy of who he was, not what he possessed. Similarly, the possessions of Abraham are lost to history, but who he was—a person of faith—remains. We become heirs of the promise in the same way when we claim Christ by our faith.

Prayer: *Gracious God, thank you for the invitation to become your heirs. Like Abraham, we profess faith in you. And we give thanks for Jesus Christ, Saviour and Lord. Amen*

Thought for the Day: The best legacy any of us can leave is faith in God.

Steve Harper (Florida)

Healing for Body and Spirit

Read Revelation 22:1–7

[The servant] was wounded for our transgressions, he was bruised for our iniquities: the chastisement of our peace was upon him; and with his stripes we are healed.

Isaiah 53:5 (KJV)

Fifty years ago, I had the opportunity to preach the gospel in remote villages with an evangelist who trained me. Along with preaching, we taught the people how to take care of their health and gave them tips for good hygiene.

One of the people who heard us asked me, 'What is your contribution in this healing ministry?' This question stays in my memory. Some might think that preaching has little to do with health and healing, but the vision of wholeness found in the Bible includes both physical healing and salvation.

This is part of God's ongoing work. Revelation 22:1–7 offers a vision of the tree of life, and 'the leaves of the tree were for the healing of the nations' (v. 2). The world needs to hear the scripture's message about healing and the place of healing. Jesus Christ who healed people's physical diseases also offers cure and comfort for our souls.

In our world full of tension, terrorism and violence, the Lord Jesus Christ invites every person to experience healing and comfort. That is why Jesus calls to all the world, 'Come unto me all ye that labour and are heavy laden, and I will give you rest' (Matthew 11:28).

Prayer: *Dear God, let us experience your healing and comfort in all the circumstances of our lives. Make us instruments of healing and comfort for others through your love. Amen*

Thought for the Day: Christ offers healing for both body and spirit.

G.V. Savariroyan (Tamil Nadu, India)

Christian Friends

Read Matthew 11:28–30
Bear one another's burdens, and in this way you will fulfil the law of Christ.
Galatians 6:2 (NRSV)

My wife and I were driving home from her last chemotherapy treatment. As I turned onto our street, I could see a large number of people in our front garden. They were holding balloons and signs, and ringing bells. As we got closer, I saw that they were members of our church family. These Christian friends had stood by us in many ways over the preceding eight months. Cards, words of encouragement, meals that were waiting when we returned from treatments—these were just a few of the ways they had helped us to bear our burden. Now these friends were seeing us across the finish line with a great celebration.

In today's scripture, Jesus tells us when we are weary to bring our burdens to him and he will lighten our load. These wonderful friends have been the hands and feet of Christ by standing with us, bearing our burden and lightening our load. Thanks be to God for the church!

Prayer: *Thank you, Lord Jesus, for Christian friends who stand by us in difficult times. Make us all aware of those whose burdens are heavy, so that we can be your helping hands and feet. Amen*

Thought for the Day: If we look, we will see people who need our help with their burdens.

Chris McCormick (Texas)

Small Group Questions

Wednesday 5 May

1. In terms of your emotional response, how does the image of a lighthouse as a witness compare to the image of a street preacher? What associations do you make that determine your response to each of them?

2. Who has been a lighthouse to you in a stormy time in your life? What did that person or those persons do or say that makes you say this?

3. In what ways can we be 'the hope of the Lord made visible' and audible?

4. How would you describe 'the safe harbour that Christ offers'?

5. Make a list of your congregation's activities that draw the most people. Look at each to decide whether it mostly illumines the inside of your building or mostly takes Christ's light outside the building. Is there balance between the two categories? Should there be?

6. When have you acted as a Christian guide for someone else? Were you comfortable in that role? Why or why not?

7. When have you found your role as Christian guide to be 'wearing and lonely'? What has strengthened and encouraged you in this role?

Wednesday 12 May

1. Whom do you consider a 'champion' at prayer? What makes you say this? Why or how might these people be intimidating?

2. How do you feel about your practice of prayer? Do you pray as often and as well as you think you should? Where does your model for the 'right' way to pray come from?

3. What is your earliest memory about prayer? What feelings are connected to that memory, and why?

4. Which honest images or requests from prayers in the book of Psalms do you find troubling or difficult to understand?

5. What is your favourite image for God and how he acts in our lives? How do all of our favourite words and images limit God?

6. What does scripture say about the way prayers should—or shouldn't—be? What does the Bible teach us about prayer?

7. Describe how your prayer life has changed. In what ways do you pray differently now from when you began your faith journey?

Wednesday 19 May

1. Do discussions that use scripture as a rulebook or weapon to prove our views misuse scripture? If so, how?

2. Read aloud 1 Peter 3:15–16. What practical guidelines about discussing our faith can we draw from this passage?

3. Should Christians study other faiths? Why or why not?

4. If Jesus lived in your community, where would he attend church and why? Would you attend with him?

5. Do you believe people with different beliefs from yours can love God as much as you do? Could they love God more than you do? What makes you say this?

6. Read aloud 1 John 4:1–8 and 14–16. How do these passages challenge us regarding our responses to those of other beliefs and other faiths?

7. Do you agree that Margie's friend does not have the right to question her faith and/or salvation? If not, why not? Would this principle apply if her friend were Christian and she were Buddhist or Hindu or Muslim? Why or why not?

8. Name some key elements of Christian faith that you think most Christians could agree on. Which do you think are most important to God, and why?

Wednesday 26 May

1. How often and how much should believers read the Bible?

2. What strategies have you tried for learning the Bible and about the Bible? Which ones have been most fruitful for you?

3. What three or four Bible passages should all believers either memorise or be familiar with? If you do not memorise, in what ways can you make scripture part of your life daily when you do not have a Bible in hand?

4. Give out 3x5 cards and Bibles to all group members. Ask each person to copy a favourite or important scripture passage. Shuffle the cards, redistribute them, and have each person read the card in hand. Ask the group to decide who wrote each passage and why.

5. What is your major obstacle to knowing the Bible better?

6. Do you have a daily time with God's word? If so, would you characterise it as more of 'a once-a-day dip into the Bible' or meditating 'day and night'? What is it about your study that puts it into the category you indicated?

7. To you, do Wendy's examples in the last paragraph qualify as meditating on scripture? Why or why not?

8. Is there a difference between a verse's sinking into your mind and sinking into your heart? Can you think of a passage that you relate to in your mind but not in your heart or vice versa?

Wednesday 2 June

1. What note or card that you received in the past brought you comfort or special joy? Why do you remember it?

2. If you drive and had to give up driving, what would be most difficult for you to adjust to? Whom would you call on for help if you were in that situation?

3. Describe someone you know in the later years of his/her life who has adapted to limitations to his/her ministry. What principle can you incorporate from their life? How can we know when to discontinue a ministry?

4. The verse quoted today says, 'Teach and admonish one another.' What is the difference between teaching and admonishing? Are some people able to perform one of these tasks and not the other? For which are you better suited?

5. What do you do as a Christian outside the church to make your community more loving and more just? What does your congregation do? Besides church, where else can we learn about opportunities to minister to others?

6. What unusual use of personal interests have you encountered in Christian ministries (sword swallowing, working on cars, knitting, riding motorcycles)? What ideas for your church's ministry does this discussion spark?

7. What are some positive ways to deal with frustration? Should Christians cope with frustration differently from non-believers?

8. Whom do you know who has a special ministry of intercessory prayer—praying for others? Is this a ministry that you feel called to? Why or why not?

Wednesday 9 June

1. What do you think would be the hardest part of asking forgiveness from your family? What would be the hardest part of offering forgiveness to one who returned and asked for it?

2. Do you agree with Carol that 'the ones we hurt the most are usually the ones we love the most'? If so, why do you think this is true?

3. The writer talks about being called by God to repent, to come clean about her past. How do we discern what we must repent of from our past?

4. How do you define repentance? How can we know if we or some-one else has truly repented? Do we have the right to judge the sin-cerity of someone else's repentance?

5. As a part of repenting, is it always necessary to tell family about bad choices we made in the past? When might it be wise not to tell, and why? Does deceiving those we love have long-term effects?

6. Some people fear God's wrath even though they have asked for-giveness for their sins. What would you say to someone who fears God's wrath?

7. What teachings about God make it difficult for people to feel for-given? What life experiences make it difficult to believe God forgives us? What helps us to believe we are and to feel forgiven?

Wednesday 16 June

1. When have you felt unable to see the way ahead and unsure of your direction spiritually? Who or what helped you find your way?

2. How do you experience God guiding you? Have you ever had a time when God seemed to reach into your life in an obvious way to direct you? What happened, and what did you carry away from the experience?

3. What experiences of others have helped you to understand how God guides us?

4. What Bible verse(s) do you come back to again and again for help in making decisions? Why this one or these?

5. The quoted scripture says that if we hope we 'wait… with patience'. Is being patient easy? What is the longest time you have waited for something important? What Bible verse(s) might help us to wait patiently?

6. What do you consider the biggest obstacles to trusting God? What are the best reasons to trust God?

7. What subjects do you wish the Bible gave guidance on, that it is silent about?

8. Does God welcome our questions when we face difficult moments or situations? What sustains your faith during times of adversity?

Wednesday 23 June

1. Are you one of those who serves quietly and inconspicuously in the church or one who serves in more public ways? Why do you serve where you do?

2. In addition to the ways listed in the last paragraph of the meditation, what can we do to provide for others 'a climate for growth' in the spiritual life? What can we do to provide this for ourselves?

3. What do you need in order to grow in your faith? What spiritual 'food' that others talk about positively does nothing for you? What spiritual activity always helps you feel close to God?

4. How can we help others to grow spiritually without trying to make them like us in the ways they live their faith?

5. How can we balance helping others to grow in their faith with not judging or 'grading' them? Can we ever know what another person needs spiritually?

6. Were you a late bloomer or an early bloomer in the spiritual life? Where do you see yourself in your spiritual 'blooming period'? When were you like an 'unopened bud'? How did you serve when you were a 'half-opened flower'?

7. What do you think Paul meant with his admonition in the quoted scripture to 'warn those who are idle'? Which of the tasks set out for us in these verses do you find most challenging? Which is easiest for you?

Wednesday 30 June

1. What methods or tricks do you use to help yourself remember things? Do certain strategies work better in some situations than in others?

2. What was the preacher's sermon about in the last worship service you attended? Did you intend to remember some point from the sermon? What can we do to help ourselves better remember spiritual insights?

3. In your mind, list three specific times you have seen God at work. Tell the group about one of the incidents. Did you notice God's work as it was happening or only when looking back?

4. Psalm 9:1 speaks of God's 'wonderful deeds'. What would you put on your list? How might you work these statements about God into your conversations with those near you?

5. Make a list of three people you are thankful to know and why you are thankful for each of them. How did these relationships develop? Do you see them as gifts from God?

6. What lately has excited you when you have seen God at work? How could you be more aware of God's activity throughout your life?

7. How can we help ourselves to be more mindful of God's presence in ordinary situations?

Wednesday 7 July

1. Re-read I Samuel 18:3. What is your understanding of 'covenant' in this context? Have you ever had a friend that you 'loved… as [your] own soul'? What kind of covenant did you have with this person? Did the two of you discuss this covenant, or was it merely understood?

2. Based on your understanding of this meditation, how is a 'soul friend' different from an ordinary friend? Do you think one person could be both? Why or why not?

3. Where is the line between giving someone an honest response and trying to shape that person to our ideas of who they should be or what they should do?

4. Do we ever have the right to tell others what to do in their spiritual life? If so, in what situations? If not, why not?

5. Who has given/offered you spiritual guidance? What was the guidance? To whom have you offered spiritual guidance? How did your guidance make a difference in this person's situation?

6. How does your church encourage its members to be accountable to each other? What 'sense of responsibility' do you have within your faith community? How do you live out this responsibility?

Wednesday 14 July

1. Have you done something like this woman did, giving money or something else to someone just because you felt an inner nudge to do so? How did the recipient respond? What did you learn from the experience? If you have not given in this way, could you do so?

2. What actions would reveal an 'open-handed, open-hearted approach' to life?

3. What does it mean to be 'careful' in one's generosity? How would you describe your own generosity?

4. Why do you think the widow told the family that the gift and amount were God's idea and that she was just being obedient?

5. Paul said about the Macedonian church: 'they gave themselves first to the Lord and then to us in keeping with God's will' (2 Corinthians 8:5). How can we apply this verse to ourselves?

6. Paul continued, 'just as you excel in everything... see that you also excel in this grace of giving'. How might giving be considered a grace?

Wednesday 21 July

1. Do you think all believers should sense God's presence? Are such experiences proof of belief?

2. Looking back on your life, what experiences can you identify as ones that drew you toward relationship with God?

3. Some people seem to have always had a sense of relationship with God, while others struggle, as Deanna did, to come to belief. Of the two, which are you, and what made you as you are?

4. Do you think it's possible that someone's relationship with God could become so damaged that the relationship could not be restored? Why or why not?

5. In what way(s) do you know God personally? Is 'feeling' a major component of your relationship with God? If not, what is a greater component? How does this relationship compare to those you share with your friends and family?

6. Re-read Psalm 126:3. What 'great things' has God done for you? What great things is God in the midst of doing? How do you define 'joy'? Is this joy a part of your life every day? Can we consciously seek and attain such joy?

Wednesday 28 July

1. What recent news story has moved you to pray? Why, and what did you pray for? Has God answered that prayer in any way that you can see? What will you do besides praying about this?

2. What need of someone you know is on your mind or tugging at your heart today? What would you ask God to do for that person?

3. How can we pay attention to the needs around us without becoming overwhelmed by the size and number of them?

4. What is on your 'blessings list' today?

5. What has helped you to remain hopeful during a difficult time in your life? How can we help ourselves to focus on signs of hope during our day-by-day struggles?

6. How can reading about despair in the life of a great prophet give us perspective as we respond to crisis and tragedy?

7. How could keeping a record of prayer requests be beneficial to our faith journey? What might a record like this reveal about our personal relationship with God? What might this record reveal about God?

Wednesday 4 August

1. Which sister in this meditation would friends or relatives say you most resemble, and why? Would people at work or in church say the same? Why or why not?

2. What saying or sayings do you remember hearing often in childhood? Do you use those same sayings now or avoid using them? Why?

3. Read aloud 1 Corinthians 12:4–7 and Ephesians 4:11–13. Which of the 'public' spiritual gifts in these lists do you have? How are they evident in your life?

4. Which of the 'private' or less detectable spiritual gifts do you have? How are they evident in your life?

5. The writer said, 'God delights in us just as we are.' In what about you does God delight?

6. In what ways is God like your dad? In what ways are the two different? How have your experience with and perceptions of your earthly father shaped your image of God?

7. Read aloud Ephesians 4:16. What do you see as your part in the work of God? How does this differ from what God expects from someone else?

Wednesday 11 August

1. If you were making a film of the situation in this meditation, whom would you cast as the drunk? As the fearful but friendly parishioner? In both cases, why? What would happen after this church service scene? How would the film end?

2. Is fear an illness? Is fear a sign of lack of faith? Could it be both?

3. How does being people of faith affect how we approach our fears?

4. What Bible stories of people being afraid can you think of? How did those people deal with their fears? How did God act to help those who were afraid?

5. Think about a time/circumstance when you had to face a fear. What helped you to face or overcome that fear?

6. God is love, and we are to reflect that love to others. What are some of the qualities of God's love? Which of these qualities do you reflect?

7. How might Ephesians 4:15—'speaking the truth in love, we will in all things grow up into him who is the Head, that is, Christ'—come into play if this stranger were to become a member of this church?

Wednesday 18 August

1. What do the following Bible passages tell you about passion/zeal: John 2:17; Romans 10:2; Philippians 3:6? Is passion for a cause always good? How do we know when it is or isn't acceptable to be zealous?

2. Think about the last emergency you heard about. How did you personally respond? How did your community respond to the emergency?

3. What people would you list among 'those the world injures'? Why are these people hurt by the world's ways?

4. What ministries of your church reach out to these injured and wounded people? What groups would you like to see receive more attention from your church?

5. How are you personally working to bring abundant life for all of God's children?

6. How do you think people might 'find their true worth as children of God'? Who do you define as 'children of God'?

7. In what ways is the church like an intensive-care unit? In what ways should it not be like an ICU?

Wednesday 25 August

1. What is the biggest difference between secondary school now and secondary school when you attended?

2. What challenges do teachers and teenagers in your community face? What support does your church offer to each group?

3. How do you respond to interruptions? Does your usual response reflect your Christian faith? What about your way of responding would you like to change?

4. Read Luke 8:40–56. How does this passage show Jesus dealing with interruptions? What lessons for dealing with our interruptions can we draw from Jesus' actions and attitude?

5. What is your most common annoyance—the thing that 'winds you up' repeatedly? How can you turn this annoyance into a call to prayer? What obstacles stand in the way of your doing so?

6. Typically, which energises you more often to pray—fear or gratitude? How can we channel fear and gratitude into prayer?

Bible Reading Resources Pack

A pack of resources and ideas to help to promote Bible reading in your church is available from BRF. The pack, which will be of use at any time during the year (but especially for Bible Sunday in October), includes sample readings from BRF's Bible reading notes and The People's Bible Commentary, a sermon outline, an all-age sketch, a children's activity, information about BRF's ministry and much more.

Unless you specify the month in which you would like the pack sent, we will send it immediately on receipt of your order. We greatly appreciate your donations towards the cost of producing the pack (without them we would not be able to make the pack available) and we welcome your comments about the contents of the pack and your ideas for future ones.

This coupon should be sent to:
BRF, 15 The Chambers, Vineyard, Abingdon OX14 3FE

Name..

Address ....

....Postcode..

Telephone ....

Email...

Please send me....................................Bible Reading Resources Pack(s).

Please send the pack now/ in ....(month).

I enclose a donation for £................... towards the cost of the pack.

BRF is a Registered Charity

UR0210

Subscriptions

The Upper Room is published in January, May and September.

Individual subscriptions

The subscription rate for orders for 4 or fewer copies includes postage and packing: THE UPPER ROOM annual individual subscription   £13.50

Church subscriptions

Orders for 5 copies or more, sent to ONE address, are post free:
THE UPPER ROOM annual church subscription   £10.50

Please do not send payment with order for a church subscription. We will send an invoice with your first order.

Please note that the annual billing period for church subscriptions runs from 1 May to 30 April.

Copies of the notes may also be obtained from Christian bookshops.

Single copies of *The Upper Room* will cost £3.50. Prices valid until 30 April 2011.

Individual Subscriptions

☐ I would like to take out a subscription myself (complete your name and address details only once)

☐ I would like to give a gift subscription (please complete both name and address sections below)

Your name ....

Your address ....

.... Postcode ....

Gift subscription name ....

Gift subscription address ....

.... Postcode ....

Gift message (20 words max) ....

....

Please send *The Upper Room* beginning with the September 2010 / January / May 2011 issue: (delete as applicable)

THE UPPER ROOM ☐ £13.50

Please complete the payment details below and send, with appropriate payment, to: BRF, 15 The Chambers, Vineyard, Abingdon OX14 3FE

Total enclosed £ .... (cheques should be made payable to 'BRF')

Payment by ☐ cheque ☐ postal order ☐ Visa ☐ Mastercard ☐ Switch

Card no: ☐☐☐☐☐☐☐☐☐☐☐☐☐☐☐☐☐☐☐☐

Expires: ☐☐☐☐   Security code: ☐☐☐

Issue no (Switch): ☐☐☐

Signature (essential if paying by credit/Switch card) ....

☐ Please do not send me further information about BRF publications

☐ Please send me a Bible reading resources pack to encourage Bible reading in my church

BRF is a Registered Charity

UR0210

Church Subscriptions

☐ Please send me ...... copies of *The Upper Room* September 2010 / January / May 2011 issue (delete as applicable)

Name...

Address ....

....Postcode.......................................

Telephone ....

Email...

Please send this completed form to:
BRF, 15 The Chambers, Vineyard, Abingdon OX14 3FE

Please do not send payment with this order. We will send an invoice with your first order.

Christian bookshops: All good Christian bookshops stock BRF publications. For your nearest stockist, please contact BRF.

Telephone: The BRF office is open between 09.15 and 17.30. To place your order, telephone 01865 319700; fax 01865 319701.

Web: Visit www.brf.org.uk

☐ Please send me a Bible reading resources pack to encourage Bible reading in my church

BRF is a Registered Charity

UR0210

Embracing a Concrete Desert

A spiritual journey towards wholeness

Lynne E. Chandler

'I wish I could say that I have arrived and will never have to stare into the darkness again, but I know that isn't so. I do know, though, that I have to embrace the present moment and celebrate life, whatever that may involve today. My Creator is alive within and throughout this amazing world, and has never failed to wrap me in wings of protection and comfort. There are many layers of negativity to be peeled back so that a glimpse of God's image can show through. Just as one layer is lifting, another appears to take its place. That's where grace comes in…'

This is the story of an unfinished journey—a journey that finds a path through struggle and difficulty to acceptance and peace of mind. It is the story of one woman choosing to seek serenity in the midst of struggles to adapt to a very different life, and discovering how, in the driest of desert places, God can reveal fresh water springs for the soul. It is a story shared through lyrical journal reflections and poems sparked by the ups and downs of life in a teeming Middle Eastern metropolis.

ISBN 978 1 84101 686 3   £5.99

To order a copy of this book, please turn to the order form on page 157.

Seasons of the Spirit

One community's journey through the Christian year

Teresa Morgan

'*"Watch and pray." Advent's motto is good for Lent, too. But I am too tired to pray; even the short step into silence seems a marathon. I am tempted to sit down under the chestnut tree and hope that the new life which touches it one sunny morning will quicken me too. Instead, I turn homewards. "O Lord, you have searched me and known me. You know when I sit down and when I rise up; you discern my thoughts from far away…" The desert behind and in front of me stretches for ever… We both know and can't know that Easter will come. I keep an only half-sceptical eye out for angels.*'

This book is a journey through the seasons of the year and also through the high days and holy days of the Church. In the company of saints present and past, we travel from Advent Sunday to Advent Sunday, looking for the Kingdom of Heaven and reflecting on the many ways in which God's love reaches out to embrace and transform the world. Interspersing prose with poetry, this is a book to read slowly and reflectively, stilling our minds to the rhythms of grace and opening our hearts to the peace that passes all understanding.

ISBN 978 1 84101 710 5   £5.99
To order a copy of this book, please turn to the order form on page 157.

The Circle of Love

Praying with Rublev's icon of the Trinity

Ann Persson

The painting of the Holy Trinity by Russian artist Andrei Rublev is probably the best-known and best-loved icon from the Eastern Orthodox Church. Beginning with her own experience of gazing at the icon during convalescence from surgery, Ann Persson shares her journey of discovery through some of the historic and artistic traditions of icon-painting, including a midwinter pilgrimage to the Russian monastery for which Rublev's icon was originally commissioned.

She provides a detailed commentary on the image itself to draw out its full significance, and also reflects on the Bible story that inspired the icon. *The Circle of Love* is perfect introductory reading for all who are interested in exploring the use of icons in meditative prayer, and discovering something of the spiritual riches found in that tradition.

ISBN 978 1 84101 750 1   £5.99
To order a copy of this book, please turn to the order form on page 157.

A Heart to Listen

Learning to become a listening person

Michael Mitton

Listening has become a lost art in our world, which has grown ever noisier, more superficial and stressed. We forget about listening not only to others but to God, to ourselves, to our communities—and even to the needs of our planet. If we do not listen, we cannot hope to grow in wisdom, to deepen relationships with others, or to share our faith in sensitive and appropriate ways.

This new edition of A Heart to Listen explores how, with God's help, we can relearn the essential art of listening. Michael Mitton interweaves biblical reflection with insights from many years of listening ministry in the UK and abroad. To speak to heart as well as head, he concludes each chapter with an episode from a creative story that tells of people listening and learning from one another in a challenging cross-cultural setting.

ISBN 978 1 84101 747 1   £7.99
To order a copy of this book, please turn to the order form on page 157.

Restoring the Woven Cord

Strands of Celtic Christianity for the Church today

Michael Mitton

When they discover Celtic spirituality, many Christians feel that in some sense they have come home. As they begin to explore the people and places significant in the early centuries of Christianity in the British Isles, they find an expression of faith that weaves together strands of being and belonging, worship and witness in a unique and powerful way.

Restoring the Woven Cord takes 15 leading figures from that era—ranging from Patrick of Ireland to John of Beverley—and shares something of their stories, showing their burning love for the Bible, their depth of prayer, their radical commitment to the poor and to caring for creation. Reflecting on their lives and works, we can find powerful inspiration for our own walk with God and rich resources for the ministry of the local church.

This is a revised edition of a bestselling book first published in 1995. It now includes insights on the continuing popularity and development of Celtic spirituality from Ray Simpson of the Community of Aidan and Hilda, Lindisfarne, Jack Stapleton of the USA branch of the Community, Bishop Eric Pike of South Africa and Liz Culling, Tutor in Prayer, Mission and Spirituality at Wycliffe Hall, Oxford.

ISBN 978 1 84101 800 3   £7.99
To order a copy of this book, please turn to the order form on page 157.

Growing a Caring Church

Practical guidelines for pastoral care

Wendy Billington

In every church, of every size, meeting people's pastoral needs is a core area of ministry. If leadership resources are already stretched, however, it can be an area in which it is all too easy to fall short, with potentially disastrous consequences. We may notice and feel compassion when we see somebody struggling in some way, but we also need to be properly equipped in order to offer the kind of wise and practical assistance that will start to guide them back towards wholeness of life.

Earthed in Jesus' command that as his disciples we are to love one another, this book shows how home groups can be places where people's pain and difficulties are noticed, and first steps taken to help. Writing for both group leaders and members, Wendy Billington offers valuable insights coupled with down-to-earth advice, drawing on her years of pastoral work in the community and in the local church, as well as on her personal experiences of loss and cancer.

ISBN 978 1 84101 799 0   £6.99
To order a copy of this book, please turn to the order form on page 157.

ORDERFORM

REF	TITLE	PRICE	QTY	TOTAL
686 3	Embracing a Concrete Desert	£5.99		
710 5	Seasons of the Spirit	£5.99		
750 1	The Circle of Love	£5.99		
747 1	A Heart to Listen	£7.99		
800 3	Restoring the Woven Cord	£7.99		
799 0	Growing a Caring Church	£6.99		

POSTAGE AND PACKING CHARGES				
Order value	UK	Europe	Surface	Air Mail
£7.00 & under	£1.25	£3.00	£3.50	£5.50
£7.10–£30.00	£2.25	£5.50	£6.50	£10.00
Over £30.00	FREE	prices on request		

Postage and packing	
Donation	
TOTAL	

Name _____ Account Number _____

Address _____

_____ Postcode _____

Telephone Number_____

Email _____

Payment by: ❏ Cheque ❏ Mastercard ❏ Visa ❏ Postal Order ❏ Maestro

Card no ⬚⬚⬚⬚ ⬚⬚⬚⬚ ⬚⬚⬚⬚ ⬚⬚⬚⬚ ▨▨▨

Valid from ⬚⬚⬚⬚ Expires ⬚⬚⬚⬚ Issue no. ▨▨▨

Security code* ⬚⬚⬚ *Last 3 digits on the reverse of the card.
ESSENTIAL IN ORDER TO PROCESS YOUR ORDER   Shaded boxes for Maestro use only

Signature _____ Date _____

All orders must be accompanied by the appropriate payment.

Please send your completed order form to:
BRF, 15 The Chambers, Vineyard, Abingdon OX14 3FE
Tel. 01865 319700 / Fax. 01865 319701 Email: enquiries@brf.org.uk

❏ Please send me further information about BRF publications.

Available from your local Christian bookshop.   BRF is a Registered Charity

About
brf:

BRF is a registered charity and also a limited company, and has been in existence since 1922. Through all that we do—producing resources, providing training, working face-to-face with adults and children, and via the web—we work to resource individuals and church communities in their Christian discipleship through the Bible, prayer and worship.

Our Barnabas children's team works with primary schools and churches to help children under 11, and the adults who work with them, to explore Christianity creatively and to bring the Bible alive.

To find out more about BRF and its core activities and ministries, visit:

www.brf.org.uk
www.barnabasinschools.org.uk
www.barnabasinchurches.org.uk
www.messychurch.org.uk
www.foundations21.org.uk

If you have any questions about BRF and our work, please email us at

enquiries@brf.org.uk

enter